THERE'S LIFE BEYOND RAT RACE

ESCAPE THE CHASE AND FIND TRUE FULFILLMENT ON YOUR TERMS.

SUDIP CHOWDHURY

Made with ❤ on the Notion Press Platform
www.notionpress.com

To all those who have ever felt trapped in the relentless race for
success, this book is for you.

To the dreamers, the seekers, and the souls who know there's more
to life than climbing the next rung on the ladder. May you find the
courage to step off the treadmill, embrace your own path, and
rediscover the joy and meaning that lies within.

And to my family and friends—your unwavering support and belief in
me have given me the strength to follow my own journey, and for
that, I am forever grateful.

This book is a tribute to the freedom of living authentically and the
pursuit of true happiness.

Contents

Contents

Foreword

Have you ever stopped to wonder why life feels like an endless race—always chasing the next goal, promotion, or pay-check, hoping that someday you'll finally arrive at "success"? But what happens when you get there and realize it's not what you thought? That the happiness and fulfilment you were promised seem just out of reach?

This book, *"There's Life Beyond the Rat Race,"* is an invitation to step off the treadmill and rethink what success and happiness really mean. This book isn't a guide to abandoning your career or ambition. Instead, it's an invitation to discover how you can live on your terms—where success is defined not by titles or pay-checks, but by joy, peace, and meaning. We dive into what happens when we stop chasing society's definition of success and start defining it for ourselves.

What to Expect

In these pages, we'll explore topics that affect all of us:

- What does real success look like? Is it about titles and bank balances, or something deeper?
- How can we find security in uncertain times? If job security is unreliable, where does true stability come from?
- What brings lasting joy and fulfilment? How do we focus on what really matters without getting lost in distractions?

Through relatable stories and practical insights, we'll talk about breaking free from corporate disillusionment, reassessing priorities in mid-life, building meaningful relationships, and learning to embrace simplicity, empathy, and positivity in everyday life.

An Invitation to Live Differently

This book isn't about doing more—it's about living better. It's about slowing down, paying attention to what lights you up, and letting go of what no longer serves you. The goal isn't to abandon ambition—it's to realign it with what truly makes life meaningful.

If you've ever felt trapped in the race for more or wondered if there's a different way to live, this book is for you. It's a reminder that life isn't about how fast you run—it's about finding joy in the journey. There's life beyond the rat race, and it's waiting for you to discover it.

Acknowledgements

This book is a reflection of the countless human interactions that have quietly shaped my perspective. I've always been more of an observer in social settings—fascinated not just by what is said, but by what's left unsaid. Body language, subtle gestures, and the stories behind the words captivate me. It's through these observations, whether with friends, colleagues, or neighbors, that I've learned the most. Some of you have inspired me with your authenticity, sharing glimpses of your true selves, and for that, I am deeply grateful.

There are also those who, perhaps unknowingly, showed me the discomfort of trying to be someone they're not. And while that often left me quiet, it also taught me invaluable lessons about human nature. This book is woven from all these experiences—direct and indirect.

To everyone I've crossed paths with, whether you realize it or not, thank you for being part of my journey. Your stories, actions, and even your silences have all contributed to the insights shared in these pages.

Prologue

There's a moment in everyone's life—maybe in the middle of a busy workday or during a quiet Sunday afternoon—when the thought creeps in: "Is this all there is?" You've followed the script, done everything right—got the degree, built a career, bought the house, and checked all the boxes. But somewhere along the way, something feels off. Life starts to feel like an endless loop: wake up, work hard, earn, repeat. And no matter how much you accomplish, the sense of satisfaction always seems just out of reach.

If you've ever felt this way, you're not alone. Welcome to the rat race. It's a cycle so many of us find ourselves trapped in—chasing someone else's definition of success, running faster and harder, hoping that happiness waits around the next corner. The truth? It rarely does.

The Wake-Up Call

For some, the realization comes after a mid-life crisis, a job loss, or burnout. For others, it's just a quiet awareness that life was supposed to feel different by now. It's in these moments of discomfort that we start to question everything: *Why am I running so hard? What am I really chasing? And is any of this even making me happy?*

This book isn't about quitting your job tomorrow or abandoning all ambition. It's about waking up to the possibility that there's another way to live—a way that isn't defined by endless hustle, promotions, and pay-checks. It's about finding fulfilment, joy, and meaning not in some far-off future but in the moments you're living right now.

An Invitation to Explore

In the chapters ahead, we'll explore what it means to redefine success, break free from corporate disillusionment, and build a life rooted in clarity, connection, and purpose. We'll talk about the courage it takes to walk away from things that no longer serve you and how small, intentional choices can transform your life.

This book isn't a guide to escape—it's an invitation to reflect, to slow down, and to reconnect with what truly matters. Because life is meant to be lived, not raced through. There's a world beyond the rat race—one filled with joy, freedom, and meaning.

You don't need to run faster. You just need to stop, breathe, and choose a different path.

CHAPTER ONE

Why Are We Always Running?

Image by ASphotofamily on Freepik

Ever feel like life has become some sort of never-ending race? Every day you wake up, hit the ground running, and by the end of it, you're left wondering, "What exactly am I running toward?" It's like you're on a treadmill that just won't stop, moving faster and faster, yet somehow never really getting anywhere. You lace up your shoes and join the race, not because you know where it's leading, but because everyone else is sprinting. It feels wrong to stop, but the farther you go, the more you question—what are we all chasing? And why?

Picture this: You're getting ready for another busy day, juggling your work, family, and all the other things life throws at you. You step outside, and suddenly, it's like the world has turned into a marathon. Everyone around you is sprinting—your colleagues, neighbours, even random strangers. They're rushing toward something, but if you asked them what, they probably wouldn't be able to tell you. The funny thing is, if you follow them, you'll eventually reach the so-called "finish line," only to realize there's no prize waiting. Just a bunch of exhausted people, unsure of why they started running in the first place.

Doesn't it sound ridiculous? But here's the thing: that's exactly how life can feel sometimes. We chase after promotions, bigger pay-checks, fancier titles, but we rarely stop to think about why. What are we hoping to find at the end of this race? Is there even an end? More often than not, we just keep pushing ourselves because we think that's what we're supposed to do. But deep down, we're running ourselves into the ground, and for what?

There's this strange belief that if we just keep going faster, we'll eventually reach some magical point of happiness or contentment. But what if we're actually missing out on the best parts of life by being in such a hurry? Think about it. The quiet moments in the morning before the world wakes up, that spontaneous laughter with a friend, or just sitting still and doing nothing at all—these aren't distractions from life. These *are* life. Yet, we treat them like afterthoughts, as if the real point of living is to reach some distant goal, when maybe the joy is right here in front of us.

We also can't ignore how the pressure to keep running affects us mentally and emotionally. Constantly being on the go can leave us feeling stressed, anxious, and honestly, pretty worn out. There's this underlying fear that if we slow down, we'll fall behind. And let's not forget the endless cycle of comparing ourselves to others. We look around and see people who seem to have it all together—better jobs, more money, bigger homes—and we feel this constant need to measure up. But even when we do hit a milestone, it never feels like enough, because there's always someone doing "better." It's exhausting.

What's really crazy is how we've convinced ourselves that this race is worth it, that if we just push a little harder, we'll eventually win. But win what? The truth is, most of us are chasing a finish line that doesn't even exist, all the while sacrificing the moments that actually matter. What if we gave ourselves permission to stop running, to take it slow, and to appreciate the journey instead of focusing on the destination? Maybe, just maybe, we'd find that the happiness we've been chasing has been here all along.

CHAPTER TWO

Life's Expectations: When Reality Has a Different Plan

Life can be a funny thing, right? We all start off with these big dreams—maybe it's the perfect career, a dream house, or a happily-ever-after story. We think if we just keep working hard, if we keep pushing ourselves, we'll eventually get there. But, life? Well, life is not just a race but a constantly changing game, where rules shift unexpectedly.

Image by freepik

Picture this: You're standing at the starting line of a race, full of energy and ambition. You're sure you're heading toward everything you've ever wanted. But as you take off running, you notice something strange. Some people zoom ahead effortlessly—everything seems to fall into place for them. They've got the career, the fancy vacations, the picture-perfect life.

Meanwhile, you're running your heart out, but the finish line? It keeps moving further away. Your pace starts to slow, and now it feels less like a race and more like you're running uphill in a snowstorm... in flip-flops.

That's when life starts throwing its curveballs. Maybe it's a job that doesn't work out, a relationship that hits a wall, or an unexpected betrayal that leaves you wondering what went wrong. You start asking yourself, "Did I take a wrong turn somewhere? Why isn't all this effort paying off?"

But here's the real kicker: What if success doesn't look like what we thought it would? What if the goal isn't to race to the finish line at all?

You see, the real magic of life isn't in crossing some distant finish line. It's in those small, everyday moments we often overlook. It's in sharing a laugh with a friend, finding peace in a quiet morning, or just taking a break to enjoy where you are right now. Success doesn't have to be a shiny trophy—it can be as simple as feeling content with the life you're living.

We all feel like we have to juggle a million expectations—our own, our family's, society's. It's like trying to keep a bunch of plates spinning in the air, hoping none of them come crashing down. But maybe, just maybe, it's time to stop worrying about what everyone else thinks.

Who says success has to be about climbing some corporate ladder or earning a big pay-check? Forget the rulebook. What if success was something you got to define for yourself? Maybe it's about chasing what *you* love, building connections that matter, or just slowing down enough to enjoy the ride.

So, how about this: Let's dream big, but also take time to appreciate the little wins. Let's laugh at the curveballs life throws, because sometimes, that's all we can do. And most importantly, let's stop letting outside expectations control what a fulfilling life looks like.

In the next chapters, we'll explore some real stories, share a few helpful tips, and definitely sprinkle in some humour—because sometimes life's too absurd not to laugh at. Get ready for a journey that'll leave you reflecting, laughing, and maybe even seeing life a little differently.

Because here's the truth: The real treasures in life aren't waiting at some far-off finish line. They're right here, in the moments you're living every day—if you just slow down long enough to see them.

Breaking Free from the Daily Grind: How to Escape the Rat Race

So, we've talked about how life can feel like this endless race that leaves us emotionally drained. But here's the good news: it doesn't have to be this way. You don't have to keep sprinting just because everyone else is. Breaking free from the daily grind isn't about dropping everything or quitting your job on a whim.

> "*True freedom starts when you begin making deliberate choices. Not to follow society's well-worn path, but to carve out a life that feels like yours.*"

First off, we really need to rethink what success means. A lot of us end up in the rat race because we're chasing someone else's idea of success—a fancy title, a bigger paycheck, or maybe even just the approval of others. But what if success didn't have to look like that? What if it meant something different for you? Maybe success isn't about climbing the corporate ladder but about having more time with your family or pursuing a passion you've put on the back burner. Defining success for yourself is the first step in breaking free.

Another thing to consider is how much of your time is spent doing things you don't actually want to do. We've all been there—saying yes to extra work, social obligations, or even just feeling like we have to be "on" all the time. It's exhausting, and the more you say yes to things that drain you, the more stuck you feel. Learning to say no isn't selfish—it's necessary. Setting boundaries is about protecting your time and energy, so you can focus on what truly matters. Maybe it's scaling back on work, or maybe it's just spending less time scrolling through social media and more time doing things that make you happy.

Image by asier_relampagoestudio on Freepik

Speaking of time, let's talk about how we can use it better. One way to free yourself from the grind is by finding multiple ways to earn money. Relying on one job for all your financial security can feel pretty limiting, especially if you don't love what you do. Maybe you've thought about starting a side hustle or learning a new skill that could bring in extra income. Whether it's freelancing, investing, or even creating passive income streams, having more than one way to make money gives you flexibility. It's like having a safety net, so you can start making decisions that aren't just about paying the bills but about living the life you want.

And honestly, sometimes the answer is simpler than we think: slow down. We're so used to hustling that we forget we have a choice. Do we really need to push for that next promotion? Or could we be happier enjoying the little things—like taking a walk in the park or spending more time with loved ones? Simplifying your life doesn't mean giving up on your dreams. It just means focusing on what really makes you feel alive, rather than filling every moment with "more" just because you think you should.

One of the best ways to find balance is to reconnect with hobbies or passions you've let slip away. Remember that thing you used to love doing but somehow stopped because life got in the way? Maybe it's time to pick it back up. Whether it's painting, gardening, or just reading a good book, making space for what brings you joy is one of the most powerful ways to break free from the grind.

Of course, none of this is easy to do alone. Surrounding yourself with people who support your decision to live differently can make a world of difference. Whether it's friends, family, or a community of like-minded individuals, having a network that encourages you to step off the treadmill can help keep you grounded. It's so much easier to pursue what really matters when you're not doing it in isolation.

"True financial freedom isn't just about numbers—it's about creating the space to grow into who you want to become."

In the end, escaping the rat race isn't about finding some magical solution. It's about making small, intentional changes that give you the freedom to live life the way *you* want. Little by little, you can start to reshape your world, not by following someone else's rules but by creating your own path. And that's where the real freedom lies.

CHAPTER FOUR

The Hidden Story Behind Success and Fulfilment

Defining Success for Yourself

We've been taught to believe that success is a race to the top—a fancy job title, a big house, a luxury car, and a bank account that never runs dry. But what if you get there and still feel like something's missing? If success is all about checking off boxes, why do so many people at the "finish line" feel unfulfilled?

The truth is, success isn't a one-size-fits-all formula. It's not about climbing the ladder faster than your neighbours or collecting status symbols like trophies. Real success is deeply personal—it's about figuring out what feels meaningful to *you* and aligning your life accordingly.

Consider this: what if success isn't about how much you have, but how connected you feel to your own life? Maybe it's about working fewer hours so you can spend more time with your kids. Or perhaps it's about following a creative passion you've neglected for years. For some, success might mean leading a simpler life, one that isn't ruled by the demands of a never-ending to-do list.

Here's a surprising realization—you get to define what success means. It doesn't have to be flashy. It doesn't have to look impressive to anyone else. It just has to resonate with *you*. Success might mean pursuing meaningful work, or it might mean having the time to enjoy a quiet coffee every morning without rushing out the door.

What's more, success isn't always waiting in the future. If we're constantly chasing the *next* thing—a promotion, a raise, a bigger house—we risk missing the joy of the present. There's a sneaky lie that says, "I'll be happy when..." But when the moment finally arrives, it often doesn't feel like enough. That's because true success lies in how you experience the journey, not just the destination.

A great way to start redefining success is by asking yourself, "What makes me feel alive?" If the things you're chasing don't bring you joy or fulfilment, maybe it's time to change course. And remember: just because the world values certain things—wealth, fame, prestige—doesn't mean you have to. The real prize is living a life that reflects your own values and priorities.

Achieving Fulfilment Beyond Material Goals

Even if you figure out what success means for you, it's only half the story. Success without fulfilment can still feel hollow. Fulfilment is what makes life rich—it's the emotional satisfaction that comes from living with purpose and meaning. But here's the catch: it doesn't come from external achievements alone.

Image by freepik

We live in a culture that tells us to accumulate more—more money, more things, more accolades. But the problem with "more" is that it never ends. Even when you reach one goal, a new one takes its place. And chasing fulfilment through material things can leave you exhausted, always running but never arriving.

Fulfilment, on the other hand, sneaks in when we shift our focus. It's not about doing more—it's about being more present in the things we already do. Think about the moments that really light you up. Maybe it's a walk with your family, a good book on a rainy day, or an evening spent with friends. Fulfilment isn't found in grand achievements—it's found in the small, everyday moments that make life meaningful.

Take Anita's story, for example. On paper, Anita had it all—high salary, powerful job, and the kind of lifestyle that screams "success." But it left her feeling empty. It wasn't until she started volunteering at a children's center that she realized where her true joy lay. She traded in her corporate career for a life that felt more aligned with her values, running a non-profit for underprivileged kids.

It's a powerful reminder: fulfilment isn't about getting more stuff—it's about living in alignment with what you truly care about. And the best part? You don't need to overhaul your entire life to experience it. Sometimes it's as simple as reconnecting with hobbies you love or spending quality time with people who matter to you.

Another key to fulfilment is giving back. There's something deeply satisfying about contributing to something larger than yourself—whether it's through volunteering, mentoring, or supporting causes you believe in. When we shift our focus from "What can I get?" to "How can I help?" life starts to feel richer.

Living a fulfilling life also means letting go of the pressure to always be productive. In a world that glorifies hustle culture, it's easy to feel like we need to be constantly achieving something. But slowing down is not a failure—it's a necessity. Fulfilment often comes in the spaces we create when we stop running and take time to just *be*.

Consider hobbies, for example. You don't need to monetize every passion or turn it into a side hustle. Sometimes the greatest joy comes from doing something just because you love it—whether that's gardening, painting, or simply taking long walks. Fulfilment isn't about results—it's about the joy of the process.

And let's not forget about the importance of relationships. We thrive on connection, and nurturing meaningful relationships can be one of the most fulfilling parts of life. Whether it's your family, friends, or a community you belong to, these connections ground us and remind us what really matters. In the end, it's the people in our lives—not our achievements—that bring us the greatest sense of fulfilment.

Finally

So, what if success isn't about the finish line at all? What if the real goal is to live a life that feels good on the *inside*, even if it doesn't impress anyone on the outside? Success and fulfilment aren't just about what you achieve—they're about how you live, every single day.

When you stop chasing society's version of success and start defining your own, you open the door to a life that feels authentic and meaningful. And when you focus on the things that truly matter—relationships, passions, purpose—you'll find that fulfilment isn't something you have to search for. It's already there, waiting for you to slow down and notice it.

The secret isn't in doing more—it's in being more present. Success isn't the end goal—it's the way you live the journey. And fulfilment? That's what happens when you stop running, start living, and realize that the joy you've been chasing has been with you all along.

CHAPTER FIVE

Escaping The Illusion of Job Security

We've all been sold a comforting story: if you get a stable job, work hard, and stay loyal, the reward will be security—a steady pay-check, promotions, and peace of mind. But here's the harsh truth: **the idea of job security is more fragile than ever.**

Image by freepik

Layoffs happen. Markets crash. Companies restructure, merge, or pivot without warning. **Even the most loyal employees can find themselves on the chopping block** when profits slip or priorities change. The security we've been promised—steady paychecks and promotions—is a mirage. But stepping away from it doesn't mean chaos. It means creating real, lasting stability, on your terms. It means **taking control** of your career, finances, and well-being in ways that leave you empowered rather than at the mercy of external forces.

Corporate Life: Glitter on the Surface

When you first enter the corporate world, it feels like a dream come true—perks galore, swanky offices, team outings, and motivational events designed to make you feel like part of a "work family." There's free coffee on tap, beanbags in the break room, and maybe even Friday happy hours. For a while, it feels like the perfect setup. But once the novelty wears off, you start to notice the cracks beneath the shiny surface.

The reality? You're not a family—you're part of a balance sheet. The company will cut costs, no matter how many late nights you've spent or how many weekends you sacrificed. Job security isn't promised to anyone, no matter how well you perform. And while they might throw in a few perks to keep morale up, those perks can't replace the unsettling truth: **corporate loyalty only goes as far as the bottom line.**

Even worse, the longer you stay in a job just for the pay-check or stability, the harder it becomes to leave. Many people get trapped in a cycle of **comfort disguised as security**—too afraid to make a change, yet too drained to continue at the same pace.

The Emotional Toll of Relying on a Job for Security

Losing a job isn't just a financial hit—it's an emotional rollercoaster. We attach so much of our identity to what we do for a living that when a job disappears, **it can feel like we've lost a piece of ourselves.** Suddenly, all those years of hard work seem to mean nothing.

Confidence takes a nosedive, and you're left questioning whether you ever really had control in the first place.

But maybe that's where the opportunity lies—**in realizing that real security doesn't come from the outside.** It's about building an inner sense of stability so you aren't dependent on a job title or a monthly pay-check to feel okay.

Creating Your Own Safety Net

So, if job security isn't real, how do you protect yourself? **By building multiple sources of stability.** Think of it like spreading your weight across several stepping stones rather than balancing on a single wobbly plank.

Diversify Your Income

Don't rely solely on your job to fund your entire life. Explore freelancing, consulting, investments, or a side hustle you're passionate about. Whether it's real estate, teaching a skill online, or something creative, having multiple streams of income gives you options. **If one door closes, others will already be open.**

Build an Emergency Fund

Think of savings as your personal safety net—a buffer that buys you time and peace of mind if things go south. You don't need to have everything figured out immediately, but knowing you've got a financial cushion gives you the freedom to make decisions from a place of strength rather than panic.

Keep Growing and Learning

The corporate world changes fast, and the skills that got you here may not carry you forward. **Adaptability is the new job security.** Stay curious. Learn new skills, follow industry trends, and build connections outside of your current role. **The more prepared you are to pivot, the less dependent you become on any single job.**

Taking the Leap: Thriving Through the Transition

Stepping away from a traditional job—or being pushed out unexpectedly—can feel like freefall. You've left behind structure, predictability, and the comfort of a regular paycheck. But here's the thing: **uncertainty isn't always a bad thing**—it's where growth happens.

The key to thriving through this transition is to **give yourself permission to go slow.** You don't have to figure out your next big move right away. Start with small, intentional steps.

Rebuild your daily routine, set new goals, and explore things that excite you.

Ramesh's story is a great example. After being laid off from his corporate job, he spent the first few weeks feeling lost and angry. But then something shifted. Instead of rushing to find another job just like the one he'd lost, he decided to explore new interests. He began consulting part-time, experimented with stock trading, and even volunteered at a non-profit. Bit by bit, he built a life that felt more aligned with his values—and realized that the layoff wasn't the disaster he'd feared. It was a new beginning.

Transitions are hard, but they're also full of possibility. You get to rethink what you want your life to look like, and you have the chance to build it on your own terms. The fear of failing is normal, but staying stuck in a situation that doesn't fulfil you is far worse.

Breaking Free from the Illusion of Corporate Loyalty

It's easy to feel safe within the walls of a company, surrounded by familiar routines. But don't mistake comfort for security. **True security isn't about staying in one place—it's about having the freedom to move when things change.**

Think of corporate life like a treadmill. No matter how fast you run, you're still in the same place. But the moment you step off, **you realize there's a whole world outside.** The perks and pay-checks that once kept you running start to feel less important, and you begin to focus on what really matters—your time, your passions, and the relationships that bring meaning to your life.

Redefining What Success and Security Look Like

What if success wasn't about climbing the ladder? What if it was about **having the freedom to spend your time the way you want**? What if security didn't mean a steady pay-check, but knowing you had the skills, support, and mindset to handle whatever comes next?

Leaving behind the illusion of job security means letting go of old definitions of success and stability—and embracing a new one. It's about building a life where **your well-being doesn't depend on a company's quarterly results.** It's about creating flexibility, setting boundaries, and choosing work that feels meaningful, not just profitable.

And the best part? Once you stop chasing the illusion, **you start building something real.** You begin to see that security isn't something an employer gives you—it's something you create for yourself. And that kind of security? **It's worth more than any pay-check.**

Finally

Escaping the illusion of job security isn't about walking away from work altogether—it's about **taking control of your career, your time, and your choices.** It's about knowing that you're more than a job title and that your value doesn't depend on a company's approval.

When you build a life that gives you the freedom to pivot, explore, and grow, you stop fearing change and start welcoming it. The world outside is full of possibility. **And once you step out, you'll wonder why you ever stayed on for so long.**

CHAPTER SIX

The Path to Self-Worth and Beyond Comparison

It's funny how we all fall into the same trap, isn't it? We spend so much of our lives looking at what other people have, what they're doing, and comparing it to our own lives. You scroll through social media, see a friend getting promoted or buying a new car, and suddenly, you feel like you're behind. It doesn't even matter if you were having a perfectly good day—one glance at someone else's highlight reel, and boom, you're questioning your own choices, wondering why you don't have what they do.

Image by wayhomestudio on Freepik

But the thing is, comparison is such a sneaky thief of happiness. We all do it, even though we know, deep down, it doesn't actually help us. It only leads to this endless cycle of stress and dissatisfaction. It's almost like running a race where the finish line keeps moving. You get close, but then you see someone else who seems to be running faster or further, and you feel like you're not enough. So you push harder, only to realize that no matter how fast you run, someone will always seem ahead. And it's exhausting, isn't it?

What's strange is how we allow these comparisons to define how we feel about ourselves. Instead of appreciating what we have or recognizing our own progress, we start measuring our worth based on someone else's life. But here's the thing: no matter how successful or happy someone seems from the outside, you don't really know what's going on behind the scenes. Everyone has their own struggles, doubts, and insecurities—they just don't post them online for everyone to see.

It's easy to forget that life isn't meant to be a competition. There's no prize for keeping up with everyone else, and honestly, what works for one person might not even make sense for you. It's like trying to wear someone else's shoes—they might look nice, but they're probably uncomfortable and don't fit you at all.

So why do we do it? Why do we compare ourselves to others when we know it only makes us feel worse? Part of it, I think, comes from this idea that success and happiness are things we can measure in tangible ways—by how much money we make, how big our house is, or how many vacations we take. But those things, while nice, aren't really what make life meaningful. They don't define who we are.

The real issue is that when we constantly look outside ourselves for validation, we lose touch with our own sense of worth. We start believing that our value comes from what we achieve, or worse, from how our achievements stack up against other people's. It's no wonder we feel so stressed all the time. We're trying to prove ourselves based on standards that don't even belong to us.

What if, instead of looking outward, we started looking inward? What if we stopped basing our worth on external things and focused on what really matters to us personally? The truth is, self-worth doesn't come from having a fancy title or a bigger pay-check. It comes from understanding who you are and what you care about, completely independent of what anyone else is doing.

When we let go of comparison, we open up space to connect with our true selves. We start to realize that our value isn't tied to external achievements—it's tied to how we live our lives, how we treat people, and how we show up every day. It's in the kindness we offer, the passions we pursue, and the relationships we nurture.

And here's the best part: when you stop comparing yourself to others, you actually feel lighter. You no longer carry the weight of trying to keep up with someone else's journey. You can finally focus on your own path and appreciate the unique experiences that make your life meaningful. You begin to see that success doesn't have to look like someone else's—it can be as simple as finding joy in the everyday moments, feeling content with where you are, and knowing that you're enough just as you are.

There's so much freedom in letting go of comparison. Imagine waking up every day without the pressure to compete or prove yourself to anyone else. Imagine feeling at peace with your own choices, not because they measure up to someone else's, but because they align with what matters to you. That's where true self-worth comes from—recognizing that your life has value, not because of what you've achieved compared to others, but because of who you are at your core.

The reality is, we're all on our own journeys, and what makes one person happy won't necessarily work for another. The more we try to measure ourselves against others, the more we miss out on what makes our own lives special. When we stop focusing on what others have or what they're doing, we finally start to see the beauty in our own path. We begin to realize that we don't need to be anyone but ourselves to feel whole and worthy.

So the next time you catch yourself comparing your life to someone else's, pause for a moment. Remind yourself that their journey is theirs, and yours is yours. It's okay to admire others and be inspired by their successes, but that doesn't mean you need to follow their path. Your worth isn't tied to anyone else's timeline or achievements. It's already within you, waiting for you to recognize it.

Once you let go of the idea that you have to measure up to anyone else's standards, you'll start to find real happiness—the kind that isn't dependent on external validation, but that grows from knowing who you are and what you truly value. And when you do that, you'll discover that life feels a lot more peaceful, a lot more joyful, and a lot more fulfilling.

Defining Your Vision of a Fulfilling Life

Ever notice how some people seem to walk through life with this quiet sense of ease, like they've figured out what truly makes them happy? They aren't stressed about keeping up with others or chasing the next big thing. Instead, they seem content, living life on their own terms. What's their secret? Well, it usually comes down to one simple thing—they've taken the time to figure out what they really want. They've gotten clear about what makes their life fulfilling.

Image by mdjaff on Freepik

It's easy to feel a little lost when someone asks, "What do you really want out of life?" It can feel like standing at the edge of a big forest without a map. But don't worry, it doesn't have to be overwhelming. In fact, it can be kind of fun if you think of it this way: Think of your life as a garden—you choose what to plant and nurture. Whether it's relationships, passions, or dreams, the seeds you tend to shape your path to fulfillment. Maybe you want a garden filled with bright, colorful flowers—things that bring you joy, like creative projects or passions. Or maybe you're more focused on practical things, like building financial security or having a steady, meaningful job. The important part is deciding what *you* want to plant, not what others think you should. The more you focus on what makes you feel alive, the more your life will thrive, just like a garden that's carefully tended.

Take Anita's story. From the outside, she had the perfect life—a great salary, a high-powered job as a corporate lawyer, and everything that screams success. But deep down, something was missing. She wasn't happy. It wasn't until Anita took a step back and asked herself what truly mattered that things began to shift. She realized that while she enjoyed helping people, her job wasn't doing that in the way she cared about. What really lit her up was working with children and helping them learn. Today, she runs a non-profit that helps young girls in need with their education. It didn't happen overnight, but when she figured out what really mattered, she started planting the right seeds, and now her life is full of purpose and growth.

Funny how we sometimes get caught up in doing what we think we *should* be doing—climbing the ladder, earning more, collecting achievements—without ever stopping to ask if we even want those things. One way to get clear on what you truly want is by looking at every decision through the lens of your values. Think of it like wearing a special pair of glasses that help you see things clearly. For every big decision, ask yourself: does this move me closer to the life I want, or is it pulling me in the wrong direction?

Rajan, for example, was a marketing manager when he got a big job offer in another city. It came with a great paycheck and a fancy job title, but also longer hours and less time with his family. Everyone told him he'd be crazy not to take it. But Rajan knew what he valued most—spending time with his family and having a balanced life. So, he turned down the offer, stayed where he was, and focused on what really mattered to him. Sometimes, walking away from what looks like a great opportunity is the best decision, especially if it doesn't fit with the life you want to build.

The thing about life is, you don't need to have it all figured out right away. It's more like an experiment. You try things out, see what fits, and adjust as you go. Priya is a great example of this. She worked as an accountant for years, and while she didn't hate her job, she didn't love it either. One day, just for fun, she signed up for a photography class. It turned out to be more than just a hobby. She started doing small freelance photography gigs on weekends, and over time, it became clear that photography was where her heart was. Now, Priya is a full-time travel photographer, and she's never been happier. She didn't quit her accounting job on day one—she tried things out, took small steps, and let her new passion grow slowly. If you're unsure about making a big change, that's okay. Start with something small. Take a class, explore a hobby, or volunteer. Sometimes the best way to figure out what you really want is to try out a few things and see what sticks.

If you still feel stuck, try this: close your eyes and imagine your perfect day. What are you doing? Where are you? Who's with you? This exercise isn't about imagining a life of luxury, but about getting a sense of what makes you feel happy and at peace. When Mallica did this, she realized her perfect day wasn't packed with meetings and business trips. Instead, she imagined a day spent writing in the morning, gardening in the afternoon, and sharing dinner with family in the evening. That vision helped her see she needed more simplicity and freedom in her life. She switched to freelance work, which gave her the time to do what she loved.

It's amazing how much can change when you start making decisions that line up with your vision for your life. But remember, you don't have to do it all by yourself. The people you surround yourself with make a big difference. There's a saying: "You are the average of the five people you spend the most time with." If the people in your life are constantly chasing things that don't matter to you, it's easy to get pulled into that same race. But if you spend time with people who are on the same journey—who support and inspire you—it's so much easier to stay focused on what matters to you.

That's exactly what Mohan did. He worked in a corporate job for years but always felt like he wanted something more creative. Then, he started attending meetups with entrepreneurs and creatives in his city. Being around like-minded people gave him the push he needed to leave his job and start his own graphic design business. Today, he's living a life that's much more in tune with his passions.

Figuring out what a fulfilling life looks like isn't something you can do in a single afternoon. It's a process, but the more you explore, the clearer it becomes. It's like having a great conversation with yourself—one that sparks curiosity and helps you see new possibilities. The best part? There's no right way to do it. It's all about what works for you. So, take your time, try new things, and don't be afraid to let your vision change as you grow.

In the end, it's not about having all the answers. It's about staying open, curious, and willing to explore what makes you feel alive. And just like a well-tended garden, your life will start to bloom when you focus on planting what really matters.

• 34 •

CHAPTER EIGHT

Being in the Right Place, in the Right Time and with the Right People

Success is like cooking a meal. It's not just about talent—it's about having the right ingredients, knowing when to add them, and surrounding yourself with the right people to share it with. Sure, hard work is important, but the combination of being in the right place, at the right time, and surrounded by the right people can really turn things around. Imagine trying to make a dish without the right recipe; even the best ingredients won't get you very far. The same is true for life. When these three factors align, they create the kind of opportunities that make everything else easier.

Image by freepik

Let's start with the idea of being in the right place. Think of it like planting a sapling. You can give it water and sunlight, but if the soil is rocky, it won't grow the way it should. Being in the right environment can make all the difference. Take Meena's story. She was passionate about fashion but grew up in a small town where there weren't many opportunities in that field. She knew she had to move to a bigger city, so she packed her bags and headed to Mumbai, where the fashion world was buzzing. Suddenly, she found herself surrounded by designers, fashion shows, and people who inspired her. Being in the right place gave her the room to grow in ways she never imagined.

But timing is also key. Think about trying to harvest mangoes that aren't ripe yet. No matter how hard you try, they just won't taste right. But if you wait for the right moment, everything falls into place. The same goes for life's opportunities. For example, look at how renewable energy is gaining momentum today. Amit, an environmental enthusiast, saw this coming years ago. While most people were focused elsewhere, Amit started learning about solar panels and wind energy. Now, with governments pushing for greener solutions, he's perfectly positioned to make a mark. His timing couldn't have been better.

And then, of course, there are the people around you. Imagine trying to win a tug-of-war with people pulling against you instead of with you. It's tough. But when you have the right team, everything feels more manageable. Arjun had big dreams of starting his own business but didn't know where to begin. He found a mentor who had been through the same struggles and learned from his experience. This mentor opened doors and provided advice that Arjun wouldn't have found anywhere else. Surrounding yourself with the right people is like having a support system that gives you strength when you're unsure.

The magic really happens when these three factors—place, time, and people—all come together. Ramesh's story shows how powerful this combination can be. He grew up in a small village with little access to technology, but he was passionate about coding. He spent hours at the local cyber cafe, teaching himself how to code. He knew he needed a better environment, so he saved every rupee he could and moved to Bengaluru, where tech opportunities were booming. There, he met like-minded people, joined coding competitions, and eventually landed an internship that turned into a full-time job with a top tech company. It wasn't just luck—it was the right place, right time, and right people all coming together.

What's exciting is that you don't have to wait for luck to strike. You can create your own opportunities. It's like getting ready for a cricket match—you don't know when the winning shot will come, but if you're on the field, bat in hand, and prepared, when the ball comes your way, you'll be ready to hit it. Whether you're still figuring out what you want to do or already working towards it, keep yourself in the game. Position yourself in environments that inspire you, surround yourself with people who lift you up, and be aware of the moments that matter. When the right place, time, and people come together, amazing things can happen.

CHAPTER NINE

The Real You: How Money and Wealth Bring Out Your True Colours

You've probably heard the phrase, "Money changes people." It's one of those age-old debates that still pops up in conversations. Some folks swear that as soon as you get a bit of wealth, you turn into someone else. Others argue that money doesn't really change you at all—it just pulls back the curtain and reveals who you've been all along. So, what's the deal? Does money really have the power to mess with your personality?

Well, here's one way to look at it: it's not necessarily the money itself that changes a person, but what it removes—the need to wear a mask. Think about it—when someone's struggling financially, they often feel pressured to "put on a brave face." They might try to keep up appearances, pretending everything's fine even when they're barely holding it together. It's a bit like wearing a mask, one that helps them blend in and avoid the harsh spotlight of pity or judgment.

Image by ASphotofamily on Freepik

Now, imagine that same person suddenly finds themselves financially comfortable. Maybe they land a high-paying job, hit the jackpot, or inherit some wealth. With that cushion of security, the need for the mask disappears. They don't feel like they have to pretend anymore. And that's when their true self starts to show up. It's not that the money turned them into someone else—it just gave them the freedom to be more of who they really are.

For some people, this can be a wonderful thing. Maybe deep down, they're generous, kind, and full of good intentions. When they finally have the financial means, they're able to share their wealth with others, support causes they believe in, or simply live in a way that reflects their values. In this case, money becomes a tool to amplify the good that's always been there. It's like shining a spotlight on their best qualities.

But it's not always a fairy tale. For others, wealth can highlight the not-so-pretty side of their personality. Ever notice how some people, after getting rich, start acting more entitled, greedy, or disconnected from those around them? They might start treating people differently, prioritizing stuff—cars, houses, status—over genuine relationships. It's easy to point fingers at the money, but those traits were likely simmering beneath the surface all along. The money just gave them room to bubble over.

At the end of the day, money is more like a magnifying glass than a magic wand. It doesn't turn someone into a different person; it just makes what's already there more visible. Whether it's their generosity or their selfishness, their humility or their arrogance—money brings those traits into sharper focus.

Of course, that doesn't mean people are stuck in their ways, rich or poor. Everyone, regardless of their bank balance, has the ability to reflect on their actions and decide what kind of person they want to be. Money might give someone the freedom to act a certain way, but it doesn't force them to. We still have choices, and we're still responsible for those choices.

So, does money change people? Maybe. Maybe not. What it really does is strip away the pretense and show us who we are underneath. For some, it's a chance to let their kindness and generosity take center stage. For others, it might reveal traits they'd rather keep hidden. In the end, wealth is just a tool—it's how you use it that shows who you really are.

CHAPTER TEN

The Impact of Empathy and Positivity in Daily Life

In a fast-paced world, it's easy to get caught up in your own challenges—work deadlines, personal goals, social commitments—and forget that **small acts of kindness, empathy, and positivity can create a huge ripple effect.** We often underestimate just how powerful a kind word, a smile, or a bit of encouragement can be—not just for others, but for ourselves too.

Empathy and positivity aren't just "nice to have" qualities—they're essential for living a more connected and fulfilling life. They remind us that we're all in this together, facing challenges, joys, and uncertainties side by side. And here's the best part: **when you spread empathy and positivity, they come back to you in unexpected ways.**

The Power of Empathy

Empathy goes beyond kindness; it's the ability to step into someone else's world, even if just for a moment, and feel their struggles and joys as your own. **It's about seeing life from their perspective, and responding with care.** In a world that often values speed and results over human connection, empathy gives us a chance to slow down and truly connect with others.

In corporate life, empathy can transform the way we work. Imagine this: instead of seeing your colleagues as competitors or obstacles, you start viewing them as people—individuals with their own dreams, fears, and struggles. Suddenly, the dynamics shift. You're not just trying to "win" anymore; you're building meaningful connections. And these connections make the journey more rewarding than any race to the top ever could.

Take Ravi, for example. Ravi used to be laser-focused on hitting his career milestones, but he always felt disconnected from his team. One day, he decided to make a change. He started having real conversations with his coworkers—listening to their challenges, sharing his own experiences, and offering help when he could. **He found that by practicing empathy, his work relationships improved, and his job felt more meaningful.**

The beautiful thing about empathy is that **it spreads.** When you treat others with compassion, it creates a ripple effect—one that not only benefits the people around you but also makes your own life richer. Whether it's a small gesture of kindness or taking the time to listen, every act of empathy strengthens the web of human connection.

Compassion in Tough Times: Job Loss and Stigma

Nowhere is empathy more needed than when someone is going through a tough time—especially **during job loss.** Losing a job can feel like the rug has been pulled out from under you. It's not just about losing income—it's about **losing a sense of purpose and identity.** Unfortunately, many people facing job loss also deal with the added burden of **stigma and judgment** from others.

It's time we rethink how we respond to someone's struggle. Instead of pulling away or offering unwanted advice, **what if we simply showed up with compassion?** Sometimes, all someone needs is a listening ear—a chance to vent, cry, or just sit in silence with someone who understands. You don't need to fix their problems; you just need to **be there.**

And here's the thing: **kindness costs nothing but means everything.** When you offer genuine support—whether it's through words of encouragement, sharing resources, or just being present—it can make all the difference. Remind people that **their worth isn't tied to their job** and that setbacks are just temporary detours, not dead ends.

Also, keep this in mind: **life has its own twists and turns.** One day, you might find yourself in a similar position, needing that same kind of support. Knowing there are people out there who care can be a lifeline during tough times. **Empathy isn't just about helping others—it's about building a support system for all of us.**

Spreading Positivity: The Sunshine Effect

Positivity is like sunshine—it brightens everything it touches. And just like the sun, **you have the power to light up someone's day with even the smallest gesture.** A compliment, a thank-you note, a smile—these simple acts can make a bigger impact than you might realize.

Take Aarav's story. Aarav worked in a high-pressure office where stress was contagious. Instead of getting sucked into the negativity, he made it a point to **greet everyone with a smile** each morning, share funny stories, and compliment his colleagues whenever he could. He even brought homemade snacks to work, just to add a little cheer. Over time, **his small acts of positivity changed the office vibe.** People smiled more, worked better together, and even started supporting each other more.

Positivity isn't about ignoring the tough stuff—it's about choosing to **see the good in life, even when things are hard.** When you focus on the positive, you help others do the same. And it creates a chain reaction—one act of kindness sparks another, and before you know it, the atmosphere shifts.

Connection Over Comparison

Sometimes, we get caught up in comparing ourselves to others—who's more successful, who has the better job, who's living the perfect life. But the truth is, **comparison steals joy.** Real connection isn't about who has more—it's about **being there for each other, without judgment or expectations.**

Deepak's story offers a great example. In his community, social gatherings often turned into status competitions—who brought the fanciest gift, who threw the most lavish party. Tired of the comparisons, Deepak decided to do things differently. **He hosted a simple, no-gift gathering, focused on conversation, food, and laughter.** The result? It was one of the most memorable evenings his friends had experienced. They realized that **genuine connection matters far more than appearances.**

Positivity isn't just about spreading cheer—it's about **creating spaces where people feel valued for who they are, not what they have.** It's about lifting others up, even when life feels overwhelming, and celebrating small moments of joy along the way.

The Ripple Effect of Empathy and Positivity

When you make empathy and positivity a daily habit, it doesn't just improve other people's lives—it transforms your own. **You become more patient, more connected, and more at peace.** It's not about being relentlessly cheerful or solving everyone's problems. It's about **choosing kindness, even when it's easier not to.**

Priya, a teacher in a small town, knew this well. Many of her students came from difficult backgrounds, and she wanted to create a classroom that felt like a safe haven. So, she started a "Positivity Circle" every morning, where each student shared something good from their day. She also handed out little gifts—colourful pencils, books, handwritten notes—just to **remind her students that they mattered.** Over time, the students began supporting each other too, turning the classroom into a place of hope and encouragement.

The lesson is simple: **your actions matter.** Every kind word, every small gift, every thoughtful gesture creates a ripple effect that extends far beyond what you can see.

In Summary

Empathy and positivity aren't just fluffy ideals—they're practical tools for building a better life. **When you choose to approach life with empathy and spread positivity wherever you go, you not only lift others up—you elevate yourself too.**

And here's the best part: **it doesn't take much to make a difference.** A smile, a kind word, a moment of understanding—these small things, done consistently, have the power to change the way people experience the world.

So, the next time life feels heavy, pause for a moment. **Look for ways to spread a little light**—whether it's through kindness to a stranger, a listening ear for a friend, or simply being patient with yourself. You never know who might need that little bit of sunshine. And in spreading it, **you just might find that your own life becomes a little brighter too.**

CHAPTER ELEVEN

Mid-Life Reflections and Finding Clarity

There comes a point in life—usually somewhere between your 40s and 60s—when you stop and think, **"Is this really how I want the rest of my life to look?"** This isn't always a dramatic moment, but it can feel unsettling. Some call it a mid-life crisis, but really, it's more of a **mid-life reflection**—a time when you step back, reassess your priorities, and ask yourself some honest questions.

image by freepik

It's not just about work or relationships—it's about everything. You pause, look back, and wonder: were all those years spent climbing the ladder really worth it? Is this path still leading to the joy and fulfillment you hoped for? The career you worked so hard to build might not feel as fulfilling as it once did. The routines you've followed for years may now feel dull or exhausting. Even the relationships you've nurtured might seem different. **It's not a crisis—it's a reset.** And while it can feel unsettling, it's also an incredible opportunity to refocus on what truly matters.

When Success Starts to Feel Empty

Think about it: You've probably spent most of your life following a plan—get an education, build a career, buy a house, raise a family, climb the corporate ladder. But what happens when you get there and realize it doesn't feel the way you thought it would? You've done all the "right" things, but something is still missing. **That's when the big questions start bubbling up:**

- *Am I spending my time the way I really want?*
- *Is my career still aligned with my values?*
- *What brings me joy and meaning now?*

At this stage, **the old measures of success stop making sense.** Promotions, titles, and pay raises might not excite you like they used to. What you really crave is meaning—something that makes you feel alive and connected. This is where a lot of people start thinking about changing careers, taking up new hobbies, or simplifying their lives. It's not because they've failed. It's because **they've outgrown their old definitions of success.**

The Beauty of Letting Go

A big part of mid-life reflection is realizing that it's okay to **let go of the things that no longer serve you.** Maybe that means leaving a high-stress job for something slower and more fulfilling. Or maybe it means walking away from social obligations that drain your energy. Letting go can feel scary, but it's also freeing. It clears space for the things that truly matter.

Ramesh, for example, spent 20 years climbing the corporate ladder. He was successful by all external measures, but one day it hit him—he wasn't happy. His job, which had once been exciting, now felt like a treadmill he couldn't get off. So, he started making small changes—spending more time with his family, exploring a side business he was passionate about, and setting boundaries at work. It wasn't an overnight transformation, but bit by bit, **he built a life that felt more meaningful.**

Relationships Under the Microscope

During this phase, it's not just careers that come into question—relationships do too. You start looking at the people around you—your partner, friends, family—and asking: **"Are these connections still meaningful? Are these relationships helping me grow?"** Sometimes, you realize that you've been holding onto relationships out of habit, not because they add value to your life.

This doesn't mean you have to cut people off. It just means becoming intentional about the relationships you invest in. **You start prioritizing quality over quantity.** You look for connections that feel genuine, uplifting, and aligned with your values. It's about spending time with people who bring out the best in you, rather than draining your energy.

The Key to Living Happier: Focus on What Matters Most

With so many distractions and responsibilities pulling us in different directions, it's easy to lose sight of what really matters. **We've become so good at multitasking**—juggling work, family, and social obligations—that we end up scattered and exhausted. But **happiness isn't about doing more—it's about doing what matters.**

Imagine your life as a garden. **Not every plant needs the same care.** Some thrive with just a little water, while others need daily attention. The key to a happy, meaningful life is figuring out which "plants" in your life deserve the most care. It could be your health, your relationships, or your passions. Whatever it is, **focus on those things, and let the rest go.**

But here's the tricky part: **focusing on what matters most means saying no to things that don't.** And that's hard, especially when we're used to saying yes to everything—extra work, social commitments, or even toxic relationships. It takes courage to say no, but **it's the only way to make space for the things that truly bring joy.**

Slowing Down and Finding Joy in Small Moments

Another secret to happiness? **Slow down.** We live in a world that rewards busyness, but constantly hustling isn't the same as making progress. Sometimes, the best thing you can do is take a step back, breathe, and savor the small moments—a walk in the park, a quiet cup of tea, or a meaningful conversation with a friend.

In fact, it's often the **small, everyday moments** that bring the most joy. It's not the big promotions or fancy vacations that make life fulfilling—it's the smile of a loved one, a good meal, or a moment of peace after a long day. **Happiness isn't in the grand gestures—it's in the little things we often overlook.**

Embracing Change as Part of the Journey

One of the biggest lessons of mid-life reflection is learning to **embrace change rather than fear it.** It's natural to feel uneasy when your priorities shift, but change is a sign of growth. It's okay to outgrow old goals and dream new dreams. **You're not the same person you were 10 or 20 years ago, and that's a good thing.**

Priya, for example, had spent years working as an accountant. It was a stable job, but it never lit her up inside. One day, just for fun, she signed up for a photography class—and everything changed. What started as a hobby slowly turned into a new career. Priya didn't quit her job overnight, but she allowed herself to **explore new passions** and see where they led. Now, she's a full-time travel photographer, and she's never been happier.

Overall

Mid-life reflection isn't a crisis—it's an opportunity. It's a chance to pause, take stock of your life, and make adjustments that align with who you are now. It's about **letting go of what no longer serves you** and embracing what brings you joy and meaning.

And here's the most important part: **It's never too late to change course.** Whether you're 40, 50, or 60, you still have time to create the life you want. The goal isn't to do more—it's to do what matters.

So, ask yourself: **What do I want my life to look like from here on out? What brings me joy? Who do I want to share my time with?** Once you get clear on these answers, you'll find that the path forward isn't as daunting as it seems. You don't need to have all the answers right now.

Just take one step at a time, and let your journey unfold.

Because the real beauty of mid-life isn't in the destination—it's in the clarity you find along the way. **And with that clarity comes a life that feels truly, wonderfully yours.**

Embracing Simplicity and Generosity: The Essence of a Meaningful Life

Image by wirestock on Freepik

"Life is like a journey. We arrive with nothing, and when it's time to go, we leave the same way."

So, if we can't take anything with us, what truly matters? We often get caught up in chasing wealth, possessions, and success. But when we pause and reflect, we start to realize that the real value of life isn't in these things. What makes life meaningful is how we use our time, how we avoid the trap of greed, and how we embrace simplicity and generosity.

Let's start with time. Time is the most precious thing we have, and unlike money or things, once it's gone, it's gone. We can't get it back or store it for later. Think of it like sand slipping through an hourglass; it's always flowing, whether we pay attention to it or not. When we realize how limited time is, it reminds us to be present, to really live in the moment instead of getting lost in the chase for more wealth or material stuff.

And about wealth—there's a funny illusion that comes with it. We often think that more money or more things will make us happy. It's like trying to fill a bucket with a hole at the bottom; no matter how much you pour in, it never feels full. Sure, buying things might bring a little joy in the moment, but the feeling fades, and before we know it, we're on to the next thing. It's a cycle that never ends, and instead of feeling satisfied, we're left constantly wanting more.

That's where greed sneaks in. Greed is like a pair of glasses that only let you see what you don't have. It blinds us to the good things already in front of us—our relationships, the beauty of nature, the small joys of daily life. When we're stuck in the mindset of always wanting more, we miss out on appreciating the present. We keep running after that next thing, thinking it'll finally make us happy, but it never does.

Now, let's talk about simplicity. Choosing to simplify our lives can feel like taking a deep breath after being underwater for too long. By shedding the excess—whether it's material clutter, overwhelming obligations, or constant noise—we create the space for joy, connection, and meaning to flourish. It's like cleaning out a cluttered room—you suddenly have room to move, to think, and to enjoy what's actually important. When we focus on the simple things—like spending time with loved ones, enjoying a quiet moment, or doing something we're passionate about—we start to feel more present and fulfilled.

Generosity is another big part of a meaningful life. There's something magical about giving. Whether it's our time, our resources, or just a helping hand, acts of generosity create a ripple effect. It's like tossing a pebble into a pond—the ripples spread far beyond where the pebble lands. When we give, we not only make someone else's life better, but we also feel a sense of purpose and connection ourselves. Giving reminds us that we're part of something bigger than just our own wants and needs.

In the end, life isn't measured by what we own or how much we can accumulate. It's measured by the impact we have on others, the connections we make, and the values we live by. Think of your life like a book—not one that's filled with a list of things you've bought, but with stories of kindness, relationships, and the moments where you made a difference. Those are the things that will outlast us, the legacy we leave behind.

So, how does all of this connect to the idea of stepping out of the rat race? Well, the rat race is all about running after more—more money, more success, more recognition. But once we shift our focus to what truly matters—time, simplicity, generosity—we realize we don't need to run at all. True fulfilment doesn't come from getting ahead in the race. It comes from slowing down, appreciating the moment, and making life meaningful not by what we take, but by what we give. When we prioritize these things, we step off the treadmill and start living a life that's rich in the ways that really count.

CHAPTER THIRTEEN

Beyond The Rat Race There are New Beginnings

Image by freepik

How about starting fresh, trying something new in life? It's exciting, right? But let's be honest—also a bit terrifying. That first step into something unfamiliar can bring up all sorts of questions: *What if it doesn't work out? What if I fail?* But here's the thing about new beginnings—they're like blank canvases, just waiting for you to paint whatever you want on them. Sure, there's fear, but there's also this incredible opportunity to create something different, something exciting.

Imagine standing at the start of a wide-open road, with endless paths stretching out in front of you. You could keep walking the same path you've always known, or you could take a deep breath, step off that familiar track, and wander into the unknown. It's a little intimidating, but isn't that where the magic happens? The thrill is in not knowing what's next, in giving yourself permission to take risks, to shake off the old patterns, and to explore something new. It's like opening a door you've always been curious about but never dared to step through.

And with new beginnings, there's a kind of vulnerability we have to embrace. We let ourselves be open to change, to growth, and maybe even to failure, but that's all part of evolving, isn't it? When you start fresh, it's like hitting the reset button. You get to leave behind the habits, beliefs, and routines that have been holding you back, and step into something that feels more aligned with where you want to go. It's freeing in a way, like letting go of an old, worn-out coat and putting on something that fits better, feels lighter.

One of the best ways to embrace this fresh start is through creativity. You know how some people say art is like therapy? It really is. Whether it's writing, painting, music, or photography, being creative lets you dive into parts of yourself that often get lost in the everyday rush. Think about it—when was the last time you did something just for the fun of it, without worrying about how good it was going to be? That's what creativity is all about. It's not about being perfect; it's about playing, experimenting, and discovering new things. No pressure, just pure exploration.

Have you ever thought about trying something new, like painting or writing? Maybe you've always been curious but never actually gave it a shot because you thought, *Oh, I'm not talented enough.* But that's the beauty of creativity—it doesn't ask for perfection, it just asks for your presence. Show up, pick up a brush, or start writing that story you've been thinking about, and see where it takes you. You might surprise yourself. Maybe you'll discover a hidden talent for sketching or realize you've got a way with words. The point is, you won't know until you try.

What's really cool is that every time you try something new, you learn a little more about yourself. It's like discovering hidden gems you didn't know were there. Every new skill or passion you uncover adds layers to who you are. And sometimes, it's in those creative moments that you feel most connected to your true self. It's like unlocking a treasure chest of potential that's been there all along, just waiting for you to open it.

Creativity can also be incredibly healing. When you get into that flow of creating—whether it's painting, writing, or playing an instrument—you kind of forget about everything else. The stress, the worries, the endless to-do lists—they all fade away. You're just there, in the moment, letting your imagination roam free. There's something peaceful about it, like you've found a quiet corner of the world where nothing else matters. It gives you space to breathe, to let go of the tension that builds up in day-to-day life. In those moments, you feel grounded, like you've tapped into something that brings you a sense of calm and clarity.

The best part? There are no rules in creativity. You don't have to get it right the first time—or ever, really. It's not about being the best or impressing anyone. It's about finding joy in the process, in letting yourself be curious. Every brushstroke, every word, every note is a small step into the unknown, and that's what makes it exciting. You get to create something that's uniquely yours, without anyone else's expectations hanging over you.

So, when you're standing on the edge of a new beginning—whether it's starting a new project, a career change, or even a personal transformation—take a deep breath and step forward with an open heart. It doesn't matter if you don't know exactly where you're headed. The beauty is in the journey, in the exploration of what's possible. And sure, there might be a few stumbles along the way, but isn't that part of the fun? The road ahead is full of possibilities, and the only way to discover what's waiting for you is to take that first step, no matter how small.

Starting something new doesn't have to be perfect. It just has to be yours. So go ahead, explore those paths, pick up that brush, write that story, or try whatever has been calling to you.

"Who knows what incredible things are waiting for you to discover when you let go of the fear and simply begin?"

CHAPTER FOURTEEN

Fine Art of Conversation – Radiate Good Vibes

Every time I get on a call with this particular person, it's the same story. The conversation swings back and forth, never really settling, and never ending on a positive note. I've noticed this pattern over the years, and it's frustrating. The person I'm talking about is part of my closest circle—blood relations, so naturally, I feel concerned and want to check in. But after each call, I find myself wondering why I even started the conversation in the first place. It always leaves me with this sinking feeling, dreading the next time I have to talk to them.

During those few minutes on the phone, I can't help but feel like something's missing. There's no warmth, no tact, no mutual respect. It's like we've forgotten how to have a simple, kind conversation. It makes me wonder—have we lost the art of meaningful dialogue?

I think it all comes down to what I'd call our "natural frequency." You know how some people react in certain ways when pushed? It's like their default setting. They're wired to respond a certain way, and you can almost predict how it's going to go. There's this old fable that comes to mind, about a scorpion and a frog. The scorpion asks the frog for a ride across the river, and even though the frog is worried about getting stung, the scorpion convinces him by saying, "Why would I sting you? We'd both drown!" But sure enough, halfway across the river, the scorpion stings the frog, dooming them both. When the frog asks why, the scorpion just says, "It's in my nature."

And isn't that the truth for a lot of us? We act according to our nature, our instincts, our patterns. It's hard to change what's deeply ingrained. But here's the interesting part: while we can't change everything about our nature, we can definitely influence parts of it. Our belief system is shaped by so many things—our environment, the people we spend time with, the experiences we have. It's like we're a mix of everything we've absorbed throughout our lives.

You could call it quantum physics or even just life experience—it all boils down to the same idea. The beliefs we carry aren't just surface-level; they go deep, right down to our core. And it's said that the universe responds to what we believe at a subconscious level. Ever heard of the phrase, "You get what you believe"? It's a little like that.

I came across an interesting story a while back in a book by Robert Fulghum. He wrote about a practice in the Solomon Islands where villagers would yell at trees to cut them down. No axes, no chainsaws—just their voices. They'd gather around a tree every morning and scream at it for thirty days straight, and eventually, the tree would die and fall over. Now, I know it sounds a little out there, but think about the message behind it. Words have power. If you scream at something long enough, it starts to break down.

And that's what happens in relationships too. Poorly chosen words can do real damage. If we're not careful with how we speak to each other, we can slowly tear down the bonds we have, just like yelling at that tree. Over time, negative patterns of thinking, or even speaking, can become so ingrained that they actually start to change who we are. We end up believing the worst parts of ourselves or our situations because we've fed those thoughts for so long. It's like filling your mind with junk—eventually, it starts to poison everything else.

That's why it's so important to clear out those negative thought patterns every now and then, like cleaning out a cluttered closet. If we let those toxic beliefs sit in the back of our minds, they can start to affect how we see the world and how we treat people around us.

It all comes back to the "Law of Attraction"—the idea that we attract what we believe. If you're constantly in a negative mindset, you'll draw more negativity into your life. But if you keep your energy positive, you start attracting better things. I once heard someone say, "Radiate good vibes," and it stuck with me. It makes sense, right? The higher your energy, the better you feel, and the better things seem to happen.

Think about it like this: when you're around people who lift you up, you feel lighter, happier, more energized. On the other hand, being around negativity can drag you down. It's all about the energy we surround ourselves with. Creative hobbies, exercise, or just spending time with people who make you feel good can do wonders for keeping your spirits high. It's like recharging your batteries.

There's an old saying that goes, "Idle mind is the devil's playground." When you let your mind wander without purpose, it can easily spiral into negativity, kind of like a ship without a sail. Keeping your mind busy with good, positive things helps steer it in the right direction, away from the storm.

Every conversation is an exchange of energy. When you approach each interaction with awareness—bringing positivity and genuine curiosity—you create connections that leave both sides feeling lighter and understood. Conversations, relationships, and even our thoughts—everything has the potential to either lift us up or weigh us down. So maybe next time, instead of dreading that call, I'll try a different approach—be more intentional with my words, my energy, and see where that takes me. Who knows, maybe it could be the start of something better.

Defeating Gossip with Smiles and Diversion and a Touch of Positivity

In the world of friendships and close relationships, it's funny how easily people can get annoyed over the smallest things. Sometimes, it feels like they're just waiting for something—anything—to trigger them. Picture a group of friends casually chatting. Someone says something innocent, completely unaware that those words are about to be twisted and stretched in every direction. It's like a game of telephone, where each person adds their own version of the story, and before you know it, a harmless comment turns into a dramatic saga of betrayal and secret schemes. Humans, with their vivid imaginations, sure love to create stories.

Image by shurkin_son on Freepik

We live in a world of inferences—where we take something we hear and run with it, often far from the original truth. It's a pretty common behaviour. People hear only what they want to hear, and the rest? They either forget or warp into something else entirely. Suddenly, a simple statement like, "I prefer tea over coffee" becomes, "I hate anyone who drinks coffee." And just like that, a tiny, insignificant comment spirals into a misunderstanding that no one saw coming.

More often than not, the real cause behind all these hurt feelings is nothing more than a comedy of miscommunication. Instead of getting lost in the gossip and rumours, wouldn't it be easier to laugh at the absurdity of it all? Life's too short to be caught up in drama that's often built on thin air.

The next time you feel your emotions bubbling up over something you heard, maybe take a step back. Gather all the facts before letting your feelings run wild. Nine times out of ten, once you have the full picture, those misunderstandings disappear as quickly as they came. And instead of diving into the gossip mill, why not go straight to the source? A simple, honest conversation can clear up so much confusion. You might even laugh together about how silly the whole thing was. It's amazing how a little humour can mend fences much faster than a heavy, serious talk.

Honestly, not every problem deserves a full-blown argument. Before you spend your energy on something, ask yourself if it's really worth it. Some things are better left untouched, and some misunderstandings just aren't worth the hassle. Let's face it, there will always be those few people who live for drama. You know the ones—they love to stir the pot, passing along stories about others just to see what happens. These folks are like little chaos agents, thinking they're strengthening bonds by sharing juicy gossip, but really, they're the ones breaking them apart.

They remind me of those sneaky rumour fairies, sprinkling negativity wherever they go. It's like they've taken it upon themselves to turn harmless comments into something darker. So, how do you deal with these gossip lovers? It's actually simpler than you'd think.

One approach is to reflect their negativity right back at them. When they start with the gossip, throw a little positivity or humor into the mix. It catches them off guard. Or you can smoothly change the subject—like a master of diversion, guiding the conversation in a completely different direction. If all else fails, you can be direct and let them know you're not interested in hearing negative talk. Sometimes, a straightforward "no thanks" is all it takes to stop gossip in its tracks.

But here's the best part: the more positive vibes you radiate, the less likely these rumour-spreaders will target you. It's like surrounding yourself with an invisible shield of good energy, making it harder for negativity to stick.

At the end of the day, the best way to defeat gossip is by fact-checking before you jump to conclusions. Have an open chat with the person involved, and you'll be amazed at how quickly misunderstandings can fade away when you shine a light of truth on them. Life's so much better when we keep things simple—add in a little laughter, sprinkle in some good times, and let the rest of the drama roll off your back. After all, wouldn't you rather spend your time smiling than worrying about what someone *might* have meant?

It's all about defeating gossip with a smile, a little diversion, and a touch of positivity. Relationships are complicated enough without letting imagination run wild. Inferences can play tricks on our minds, making us believe things that aren't even close to reality. So, the next time you hear something that gets under your skin, take a step back, breathe, and maybe have a good laugh at the absurdity of it all. You'll feel a whole lot lighter for it, and who knows? You might even stop a soap opera from forming out of thin air.

CHAPTER SIXTEEN

How to Define Ourselves Beyond Labels

I recently stumbled across a line on my social media feed:

> "*You are not your job.*
> *You are not your parents.*
> *You are not your credit score.*
> *You are not your clothes.*
> *You are the sum of your words, choices, and actions.*"

Something about it just clicked. It got me thinking—how often do we let labels define us, or worse, let them define others? We meet people—neighbours, colleagues, casual acquaintances—and without even realizing it, we start to build a story in our minds based on things like their job title or the kind of car they drive.

Image by rawpixel.com on Freepik

It's like we're wired to immediately categorize people by these external markers. We say things like, "Oh, so you're the CEO of that company?" or "Wow, you're a Senior VP?" And suddenly, there's this unspoken weight placed on those titles, as if the person is more interesting or worthy of our time because of what they do or how much they make. But here's the puzzling part—sometimes, even if that person isn't particularly kind or respectful, we still put them on a pedestal just because of their status. It's like we've been conditioned to respect the label over the person.

I've seen this happen so many times, where someone with a fancy title ends up making decisions for the group, and everyone just goes along with it, trusting that their status somehow means they know what's best. But often, their decisions are far from considering what's best for everyone—they're just self-serving. It makes you wonder: how do we stop ourselves from being so easily swayed by labels? How do we really get to the core of who someone is, beyond the shiny packaging?

When we're born, we don't come with labels. We don't have jobs or houses or fancy degrees. We're just pure, unfiltered versions of ourselves, and it's the people around us—our family, friends, and society—that start shaping us. We pick up habits, ideas, and beliefs from them, both good and bad, and over time, these influences build up layers on top of our true selves.

From a young age, we're taught to admire people based on their professional success or wealth. It's all around us—schools praise top performers, the media celebrates the rich and powerful. We grow up thinking that to be "successful," we need to follow that path, and in turn, we start judging others by the same standards. We value the person with the big job or the big house, often ignoring whether they're compassionate, empathetic, or just plain decent. But what happens when we start looking beyond those labels? When we stop letting someone's bank account or business card tell us who they are?

It's like peeling away the layers of an onion. Beneath the job titles and material possessions, there's a real person with real emotions, vulnerabilities, and strengths. When we interact with others on that level—when we let go of the superficial stuff—we create connections that are genuine, built on trust and respect. And it's those connections that actually enrich our lives. At the end of the day, it's not about how many titles or accolades we've collected, but about the relationships we've built and the way we've touched the lives of others.

It's a strange thing, though, because even though we all know deep down that material things don't define us, we still get caught up in them. But here's the truth: when we're born, we don't come into this world with anything—not a job, not a house, not a reputation. And when we leave, we don't take any of that with us either. Everything we spend so much time chasing—the titles, the money, the stuff—it all stays behind. What really lasts is the impact we've had on the people around us.

Think about the people in your life that you remember fondly. It's not their job or their bank balance that sticks with you—it's the way they made you feel, the kindness they showed, or the wisdom they shared. That's what truly matters. But somehow, society has managed to convince us otherwise, and we end up placing way too much importance on things that, in the grand scheme of things, are pretty meaningless.

When we stop defining ourselves and others by labels, we start to see things more clearly. Labels are like name tags handed out at a party—they tell part of the story, but they can never capture who we truly are. Our worth lies in the values we hold, the relationships we nurture, and the joy we find in simply being ourselves. We begin to appreciate the person in front of us for who they truly are, not what they do or what they have. It makes our interactions richer and more meaningful. And on a larger scale, when more of us start to think this way, it has the power to create a kinder, more inclusive society. We stop competing over who has the flashiest life and start valuing the things that really make life worth living—compassion, empathy, connection.

This shift in perspective doesn't just help us with others—it helps us with ourselves too. When we stop measuring our worth by our job title or how much money we make, we start to feel lighter, freer. We begin to focus on what truly makes us happy, what fulfills us, and we realize that those things have nothing to do with external success.

Our worth comes from how we live our lives, how we treat people, and the positive difference we make in the world.

In the end, that's the real legacy we leave behind. It's not about the titles or the stuff we accumulate. It's about how we showed up in the lives of the people we cared about. So maybe it's time to let go of the labels and start defining ourselves by something much deeper—something that truly matters.

CHAPTER SEVENTEEN

Confirmation Bias – Why We're All a Little Stubborn

Ever found yourself in a debate about pineapple on pizza? You know, one of those arguments where everyone is absolutely certain they're right. That's confirmation bias at play—a little mental quirk that makes us see what we already believe and ignore everything else. Whether you're choosing your next Netflix show or picking a side in politics, confirmation bias works like a filter in your brain, shaping what you see and hear.

So, what exactly is confirmation bias? Picture this: You're trying to figure out if renting a house is better than buying one. You type it into a search engine, and—boom!—all these articles pop up, singing the praises of renting. "Ah-ha!" you think, "I knew renting was the way to go!" But if you'd asked the opposite question—"Is buying better than renting?"—you'd get a whole different set of answers, equally convincing, showing why buying is the best decision ever. It's not magic; it's just your brain playing favorites. And once you've made up your mind, any new information you come across somehow gets twisted to fit what you already believe.

Here's the thing: we're all guilty of confirmation bias. It's not just something that happens to other people—we all do it, whether we realize it or not. Think about it. You probably stick to news channels that match your political views, or maybe you spend more time with friends who share your opinions on big topics. We all love that feeling of having our beliefs validated. It's comforting. But the downside is that it can mess with how we make decisions and how we see the world around us.

Take the office, for example. If you're convinced someone doesn't like you, you'll start noticing every little thing they do that seems to back up your theory. Maybe they didn't smile when they passed you in the hallway or didn't invite you to lunch. Your brain seizes on these moments as proof that they have something against you. The truth might be that they're just having a rough day, but your confirmation bias is hard at work, feeding you all the "evidence" you need to confirm your suspicions.

This happens all the time, in bigger ways too. If you've decided that someone is untrustworthy, you'll see everything they do through that lens, even if their actions are totally innocent. Meanwhile, someone you like can get away with anything because you're only noticing the good stuff that supports your positive view of them. It's all about that invisible filter in your head, quietly shaping your thoughts, decisions, and interactions. And while it might make you feel secure in your beliefs, it can also close you off to new ideas and keep you stuck in your own little bubble.

Then there are those everyday conversations where confirmation bias turns something small into a heated, but completely pointless, debate. You know the kind—those discussions about whether Biden is better than Trump, or if Modi outshines Rahul. These are the kinds of arguments where everyone is determined to win, even though, deep down, we all know it doesn't really matter in the grand scheme of things. It's like two people walk into a discussion, both armed with their own opinions, and instead of really listening, they cherry-pick facts that support what they already believe. Before long, the conversation turns into a full-blown argument, with neither side willing to budge.

What makes these debates so exhausting is that they're not really about the topic at hand. They're about proving that you were right all along. That's where confirmation bias steps in, turning what could have been a good exchange of ideas into a stubborn battle to win. So, next time you find yourself in one of these arguments, maybe ask yourself: is this really worth it? Or am I just feeding my own confirmation bias, trying to win an argument that doesn't even matter? Sometimes, it's better to let it go, agree to disagree, and maybe save your energy for something more meaningful—like debating whether pineapple truly belongs on pizza.

This bias sneaks into the bigger parts of life too. Think about how it plays out in places like courtrooms, where a judge might have a gut feeling about a case, and then only pay attention to the evidence that backs up that feeling. Or lawmakers, who might be so set on their belief that they make decisions based on their personal narrative, ignoring anything that contradicts it. Even teachers can fall into this trap, presenting material in a way that pushes their own beliefs, influencing students in ways they might not even realize.

It happens in the corporate world as well. A manager might picture the "ideal" employee and only notice those qualities in candidates who fit that image, completely overlooking others who might be just as qualified. Or they might get attached to a particular strategy and focus only on the data that supports it, ignoring the signs that it's time to change course. Confirmation bias can quietly ruin decision-making, whether you're hiring, managing, or trying to steer a company in the right direction.

And it's not just in the workplace. Social media algorithms are designed to keep us in our own little echo chambers. We get fed content that lines up with our existing views, making us more divided, more stubborn, and less open to different perspectives. We feel validated, sure, but it comes at the cost of real understanding. We end up in our own bubbles, where we're always right and everyone who thinks differently is wrong.

So, what can we do about it? Well, the key is to step outside our comfort zones and seek out information that challenges our views. It might feel uncomfortable at first—kind of like wearing a new pair of shoes that need breaking in—but it's worth it. By broadening our perspectives, we can make better decisions, have more meaningful conversations, and maybe, just maybe, get a little closer to the truth.

CHAPTER EIGHTEEN

Embrace the Quirk Within

image by kues1 on Freepik

We all know someone like Atul. He's the kind of guy who believes he's the living embodiment of virtue, kindness, and a no-nonsense attitude. Atul carries himself as if the world's kindness rests on his shoulders, convinced that everyone else sees him exactly the way he sees himself.

But here's the twist—what Atul thinks of himself and how others actually perceive him are worlds apart.

In his mind, he's walking around with an invisible crown of greatness. But to everyone else, Atul's behaviour tells a very different story. You see, while Atul thinks he's charming and straightforward, his neighbours have noticed something quite different. They see someone who's dismissive, arrogant, and, let's be honest, a bit rude. It's the kind of behaviour that makes you shake your head and chuckle.

Take a scene from the local coffee shop, for example. There's Atul, sitting there, sipping his chai with that air of self-importance, completely unaware that the folks around him are sharing stories about his latest escapades. He's blissfully ignorant of the whispers about his arrogance, his unkind remarks, or how he loves to criticize others behind their backs. The people around him laugh, shaking their heads, while Atul continues to float through life, none the wiser.

It's funny, isn't it? We've all met someone like Atul—people who are so convinced of their own greatness that they don't notice the disconnect between how they see themselves and how others see them. But here's the thing: there's a little bit of Atul in all of us. We might not be as obvious about it, but we all have moments where we assume we're walking through life with a golden halo, only to later realize that our actions weren't exactly as virtuous as we thought.

Why does this happen? Why do we sometimes believe we're better than we are? Well, psychologists have a name for it—*illusory superiority*. It's a cognitive bias that makes us overestimate our abilities and our goodness compared to others. And whether we like to admit it or not, we've all fallen into this trap at one point or another.

Atul, for all his flaws, is a perfect example of this. He's mastered the art of talking the talk, but when it comes to walking the walk, he stumbles. But before we rush to judge him too harshly, maybe we should take a moment to reflect. Because the truth is, we all have our moments of "illusory superiority." We all have times when we embellish our virtues a little, or when we see ourselves in a more flattering light than we deserve.

And that's okay. It's part of being human. We all have quirks, imperfections, and little moments of vanity. What's important is to recognize those moments, laugh at ourselves, and move forward with a bit more humility. After all, humility is what keeps us grounded. It's what helps us connect with others and reminds us that none of us are perfect—nor do we need to be.

So, the next time you catch yourself exaggerating your own kindness or greatness, remember Atul. Let that thought bring a smile to your face, and maybe even a little laugh. It's a reminder not to take ourselves too seriously. Embrace the quirkiness, the absurdity of it all, and let those moments be a gentle nudge to stay humble, to stay real.

Because at the end of the day, it's those little quirks, those funny imperfections, that make us human. Our quirks are what set us apart—they're our superpower. Instead of hiding them away to fit in, let them shine. And there's beauty in that. Cheers to the paradox of self-perception and reality, and to laughing at ourselves along the way. The world doesn't need more of the same; it needs the vibrant, unique energy that only you can bring.

CHAPTER NINETEEN

Power, Privilege, Perks

Image by freepik

I can't help but smile when I think back to the early days of my career. Everything felt so new, exciting, and full of possibilities. Back then, having a company-provided laptop or mobile phone was practically unheard of. The office was filled with the clatter of desktop keyboards, the occasional ring of a landline, and the hum of old computers.

Email access? That was reserved for a select few. But because my job involved frequent international travel, I was one of the lucky ones who got a company laptop and phone. You'd think I'd won the lottery! Some of my colleagues certainly acted like they had, proudly parading their shiny gadgets around the office like trophies they had fought hard for, soaking up the admiration. You couldn't help but chuckle because, really, these weren't personal treasures—they were just tools to help us get the job done. The day we walked out of that job, the laptop and phone stayed behind, ready to be handed over to the next person.

It's funny how easy it is to get attached to these things, isn't it? If someone had gently reminded them, "Hey, that fancy laptop isn't a badge of honor; it's just a tool," I wonder if it would've changed their perspective. Maybe they'd have focused more on using those tools to do great work instead of basking in the glow of their gadgets.

That memory brings me to a recent story that's been making the rounds. Picture this: an IAS trainee, fresh out of the academy, lands a prestigious role as an assistant collector in Pune. Instead of diving into the job and making a difference, she starts making demands—fancy privileges like a beacon on her car, a luxury sedan, and an office decked out in plush comfort. It's almost like she thought she was in a Bollywood movie, playing the lead role of a high-flying bureaucrat.

Now, the Indian Administrative Services (IAS) is no joke—it takes grit, hard work, and brains to make it through the UPSC exams. But for some, once they've secured that prestigious position, the allure of power and privilege can go straight to their heads. It's like they've forgotten what the job is really about. Instead of being grateful for the opportunity to serve, they get caught up in the perks and status that come with the role. It's almost like getting drunk on your own success, and we all know how that ends—usually in a stumble, if not a full-on fall.

Here's the real kicker, though: the heart of public service isn't in the perks, it's in the service itself. The true power lies not in the privileges but in the responsibility to do something good, something meaningful. But too often, people step into roles of authority and think, *Now I'm in charge, people will come to me, and I have staff at my disposal.* They forget that the real honor isn't in the power they hold—it's in how they use it. Can you imagine giving one of these power-hungry folks a reality check? Maybe hand them a toy crown and say, "Here's your crown, your majesty. Now, how about using your 'royal powers' to actually help someone?"

It's easy to laugh at, but it's also a sobering thought. Power and privilege, if not handled with humility, can become a trap. The more we give importance to the perks, the more we lose sight of the purpose. What if, instead of getting caught up in the perks of the job, people focused on what they could accomplish for others? Imagine the difference it would make if public servants saw themselves as beacons of hope rather than status symbols. The true power isn't in the flashy car or the fancy office—it's in the difference you can make, the lives you can touch.

We often give too much credit to the external trappings of success—the gadgets, the titles, the perks—without realizing that these things don't define us. They don't make us better or more valuable. What truly matters is how we use our time, our resources, and our influence to make the world around us a little better. Power, privilege, and perks will fade, but the impact we make will last. When we focus less on what we have and more on what we do with it, that's when the real magic happens.

True Wealth: Beyond the Glitter and Glamour

I've always been fascinated by the idea of wealth. Not the kind that sparkles and shines, but the kind that you don't necessarily see right away. In today's world, it's easy to get caught up in the glitter and glamour of things—money, status, the latest gadgets. But there's a difference between people who are genuinely wealthy and those who just put on the act. It's not just about how much money is sitting in their bank account; it's about their mindset, how they live their lives, and the values they hold.

I remember early in my career, back when having a company laptop or phone was a big deal. Some of my colleagues would strut around the office, practically flashing these gadgets like they were medals they'd won. But here's the thing—they didn't own those laptops. They were just tools, handed out by the company, to help get the job done. It's funny how people can sometimes mistake the perks of their position for personal achievement. It's like walking into a fancy restaurant in a sweater vest, quietly enjoying a meal, tipping generously, and leaving without a fuss. You don't need to make a big deal out of what you have if you know your worth. The truly wealthy don't feel the need to show off—they're secure enough not to care.

On the flip side, you've got the people who walk into the same restaurant decked out in designer clothes, making sure everyone notices them. They'll complain about the smallest things, like the water not being sparkling enough, as if being fussy somehow proves they've "made it." They're the ones snapping selfies with the menu, tagging every location on social media, trying to make sure the world sees how fabulous their life looks. But scratch the surface, and there's not much going on beneath. It's like watching someone play a part in a show where the goal is to be as flashy as possible, even if it means missing out on the real experience.

It's easy to spot the difference when you pay attention. Truly wealthy people don't need to talk about their money or their possessions. They'll tell you about their experiences instead—things they've done, the places they've been, the people they've met along the way. You can feel the difference when you're with them. It's not about what they own; it's about how they live. You'll hear stories of hiking in the mountains or learning pottery in a small village, and you'll realize they're not trying to impress anyone—they're just sharing what matters to them.

Recently, I came across this photo of a race between dogs and a cheetah, and the cheetah didn't even move. When asked why, the race coordinator said, "The cheetah doesn't need to prove it's the fastest." That hit me. The cheetah knows its own strength. It doesn't need to race to show off. It saves its energy for when it really matters, like when it's hunting. And that's the thing about true wealth—people who are genuinely rich don't need to be in constant competition. They know their worth, and they focus on what's important, not on proving themselves to others.

I've always thought that the truly wealthy are the ones who live rich lives. They've got stories to tell, not because they want to show off, but because they've lived through meaningful experiences. Spending time with them is like reading a great adventure novel, one that's full of depth and substance. Imagine sitting with someone who's sailed around the world, not for the bragging rights, but for the love of the sea. They're not interested in impressing you with a slideshow of their luxury cars—they're telling you about the friendships they've made and the storms they've weathered. Their wealth is in their experiences, not in the things they've collected.

The truth is, the more we focus on the glitter and glamour, the further we get from what really matters. People who spend their lives chasing status, wearing designer sunglasses indoors, and name-dropping celebrities, might look like they've got it all, but it's often just surface-level stuff. They're playing a part, trying to convince themselves and everyone else that they're important. But when you really think about it, that's exhausting. True wealth isn't measured in possessions or bank balances—it's measured in the richness of your experiences, the strength of your connections, and the purpose that drives you each day.

What I love about truly wealthy people is that they know how to have fun, but in a way that's meaningful. Instead of throwing money around in nightclubs, they'll invite you over for a dinner where everyone cooks together, laughs, and shares stories. It's the kind of fun that leaves you feeling full, not just from the food but from the experience itself. These moments stay with you long after the night ends because they're real, genuine, and they mean something.

At the end of the day, the difference between being truly rich and just acting rich comes down to authenticity. It's about having the quiet confidence of knowing who you are and what you stand for, without needing to prove it to anyone. The truly wealthy, like that cheetah, don't waste their energy on unnecessary races. They focus on what matters, on what enriches their lives and the lives of those around them. They know that sometimes the most powerful thing you can do is simply *be*, without the need to show off or impress.

As we go through life, chasing our own version of success, it's important to remember that true wealth isn't found in glittering things. It's found in the richness of our experiences, the depth of our relationships, and the quiet confidence of knowing our worth.

CHAPTER TWENTY-ONE

INTERLUDE: A Pause for Reflection

You've journeyed through some important ideas so far—rethinking success, stepping off the treadmill of societal expectations, and rediscovering what truly matters. But before we move forward, it's essential to pause and reflect. Personal growth isn't about racing through lessons; it's about absorbing, questioning, and applying what resonates.

Take a moment to consider how the concepts in these earlier chapters relate to your own life. Ask yourself:

What areas of your life feel the richest?

Think about the aspects of your life that give you the most fulfillment. Is it your relationships? Your hobbies? The quiet moments when you feel at peace? What makes those areas rich in meaning, and how can you nurture them even more?

Where do you see yourself caught in societal labels?

Reflect on the labels others might place on you—your job title, your role as a parent, partner, or friend. Are any of these labels weighing you down or limiting your sense of self? What would it look like to step outside those labels and define yourself in more personal terms?

What definitions of success have you been chasing?

Take stock of the goals you've been pursuing. Are they truly yours, or have they been shaped by external pressures—society, family, or culture? How might your life change if you redefined success based on your values rather than the expectations of others?

What small changes can you make today to align your life with what matters most?

Consider a few small, actionable steps you can take to bring your life closer to what fulfills you. Maybe it's setting boundaries at work, reconnecting with a passion project, or simply carving out time for yourself each day. The journey to fulfillment doesn't happen overnight—it's made up of small, intentional choices.

This reflection is your opportunity to pause and reconnect with what's meaningful to you. As you move through the next part of the book, carry these questions with you. Let them guide you as you explore new ideas and possibilities. Remember, it's an invitation to reshape your life, one thoughtful step at a time.

CHAPTER TWENTY-TWO

Growing Up a Bengali: The 'Dada' Chronicles

I grew up in a quiet town far from the hustle and bustle of mainstream Bengal. Though small, our town had a significant Bengali influence, with many residents tracing their roots back to Bengal. My family, starting with my grandfather, a distinguished law professional, had moved to Allahabad from Dhaka in pre-independence days. After earning his law degree, he sought peace and solitude, eventually settling in a picturesque town in Jharkhand, then part of Bihar.

Our town was a close-knit community where everyone knew everyone. My father and his elder brother, both lawyers, were well-known figures. The people I grew up with were kind-hearted and simple. Neighbourhood disputes were rare and quickly resolved, with everyone soon returning to their usual warm greetings of "Jai Ram Ji Ki."

Growing up in a Bengali household meant being immersed in our rich cultural heritage. We were conditioned from childhood to appreciate Rabindra Sangeet and Sukumar Roy's humorous poems. My father, inspired by Netaji Subhas Chandra Bose, was an active member of a local Bengali cultural club. He organized street processions on Netaji's birthday, which we children eagerly participated in, singing patriotic songs and wearing colourful outfits.

Bengali New Year was a time of visiting each other's homes, exchanging greetings, and writing letters to relatives seeking their blessings. Rabindra Jayanti saw us children performing dances, reciting poems, or singing songs from the vast collection of Tagore's Geetanjali. We prepared for these performances weeks in advance, our homes filled with the steady presence of Bengali literature like Desh, Nabo Kallol, Sandesh, and Kishore Gyan Bigyan.

Afternoons were quiet, with my mom enjoying the sun while making aachar, pappad, or knitting sweaters. The town had two cinema halls, and we learned about new movies from a man hired by the owners who announced them in a high-pitched tone through a microphone while riding a rickshaw. We loved imitating his announcements, especially when he talked about classic Bengali films. These announcements would fill every household with joy, and the women would don their best saris and makeup to attend the screenings.

My childhood was simple. I spent my early years catching dragonflies and flying kites, shouting "Bhokatta" when I cut someone else's kite. As I grew older, I made friends and enjoyed playing cricket and football. My father sponsored a township football league in memory of my grandfather, and we spent summer days watching matches, regardless of the weather. Celebrations involved throwing whatever we had in our hands into the air, whether it was shoes or chappals.

Winter days were for cricket, and my mom insisted we bathe and apply mustard oil to protect our skin. We'd watch matches at Gandhi Maidan, returning home covered in dust and suntan, but it was all part of the fun. Load shedding was common, and TV was a new and exciting form of entertainment. We eagerly awaited evening serials or news bites, though power outages often disrupted our favorite shows, leaving us grumbling as we went to bed.

My mom frequently nagged us to study with her constant "Porte bosho" and "Eshob ki hocche." She wanted us to do well in life, but those TV moments, even with power cuts, were our escape from schoolwork and exam preparations.

Embarking on an adventure for higher education in Europe had always been my dream. The allure of the wide, wide world called to me, and I left home with excitement bubbling in my heart. After securing my master's degree in engineering, I returned home, ready to dive into the professional world.

My first job placed me in the heart of Bengal, a region rich with vibrant culture and characters. It was here that I encountered the quintessential Bengali spirit. My colleagues, most of whom were products of Jadavpur University—the so-called cultural hotbed of mainstream Bengal—introduced me to a world of street slangs and colorful personalities.

"You speak too bookishly," one colleague remarked one day, his tone half-amused, half-baffled.

"What can I say?" I shrugged. "I grew up in an environment where proper language was the norm. Your slangs sound like gibberish to me."

This exchange set the stage for countless evenings of carrom sessions, laughter, and the occasional bout of leg-pulling, which sometimes crossed the line. I rode the emotional roller coaster of those early days—sometimes content and at peace, other times stressed and overwhelmed.

A welcome change came when I took up an international assignment in Southern India, in a city known as the Silicon Valley of India. The metropolitan culture offered relief from the previous noise and cacophony. One international assignment led to another, and soon I was living out of a suitcase, hopping from one global destination to the next. I revelled in these travels, meeting new people, making friends, and exploring cities renowned for their architectural heritage.

As years passed, the desire to slow down began to nag at me. My mind itched with the thought of settling down. I remembered my dad's long-cherished dream of owning a piece of Bengal. Why not Kolkata, the heart of Bengali culture?

With help from close family members who had long settled in Kolkata, I found the perfect place and quickly dropped anchor. Little did I know, this decision would introduce me to the barrage of "dada" calls from the neighbourhood.

Initially, it was amusing to be addressed as "dada" by individuals much older than me. But soon, it began to grate on my nerves. I embarked on a painstaking research mission to unearth the hidden truths of the "dada" culture. Countless hours of observation led me to a humorous conclusion.

It was like an American Western movie where the good guy and bad guy face off with guns. In Bengal, when two strangers meet, the one who first says "are dada" wins. The other loses the plot and becomes the perpetual "dada." This is how I ended up being the universal "dada" in the neighbourhood, much to my wife's chagrin.

One day, she couldn't hold back her laughter and said, ""tomar theke boyeshe boro, aar tomai dada bolche. Lojja kore na onader? Sob tomar dosh, chule hair color lagate paro na onader moton?" (They are older than you, and they call you 'dada'? Aren't they ashamed? It's all your fault! Can't you color your hair like them?)"

I'd laugh and remind her, "Even my hero, Mahendra Singh Dhoni, rocks the salt-and-pepper look. I'm just following in his footsteps."

My life now is filled with some crazy, loud, noisy, and rather cute personalities. One friend joked that while his flight was airborne over our apartment complex, he heard high-decibel sounds through the buzzing aircraft engines from down below. Another friend immediately pointed out, "That might be because these guys were having their apartment complex meeting at exactly the same time."

Growing up Bengali meant living in a world where family, community, and education were central. Success wasn't just personal; it reflected the hopes of those around you. While this gave me a deep sense of purpose, it also brought pressure to conform to external expectations of success.

In Bengali culture, education is the golden key. Over time, I started questioning whether I was pursuing these goals for myself or to fulfill the expectations of my upbringing.

In the end, my Bengali upbringing shaped my understanding of success - it's about finding peace within, not just meeting societal expectations. I found a path beyond the rat race—one where family, community, and personal joy coexist in harmony.

And that, dear reader, brings me to the end of my story. I've realized I've grown up and am ready to face the bull by its horns. Life as "dada" has been a roller coaster, but it's also been a hilarious and enriching journey, filled with laughter, learning, and an abundance of human quirks. Ha ha!

CHAPTER TWENTY-THREE

From Picture Postcards to Pixels – A Comic Take on GeoTags and Photofloods

Remember the good old days when a postcard was the pinnacle of travel bragging? You'd pick the most exotic one you could find, scribble a quick "Wish you were here!" and pop it in the mail. That single postcard had to carry all the weight of your adventure—whether you were on a serene beach or fighting off monkeys at a temple. Simple, personal, and just a little mysterious.

Fast forward to today, and we're no longer just sending postcards. No, now it's all about *geotagged* photos and perfectly filtered shots—posted, of course, in real time. We've traded the delayed satisfaction of a postcard for the instant gratification of "likes". With every "like" we're chasing, we might just be entering a different kind of rat race—the social media race for validation.

Let's face it—social media has turned many of us into unofficial travel influencers, even if all we're doing is visiting the next city over. We snap, filter, tag, and wait... counting the hearts, comments, and emojis as if they're the currency of our self-worth. And suddenly, it's not just about enjoying the moment, but capturing the *perfect* moment—one that says, "Look at me! My life is amazing!"

But here's the funny thing: behind all those perfectly framed photos and witty captions, we can easily get trapped in a loop of appearances. We're constantly curating a version of our lives that feels more like a performance than reality. It's exhausting, isn't it? One second you're enjoying a quiet cup of coffee, and the next, you're repositioning it five times for that perfect shot. The coffee's gone cold, but hey, at least the lighting is on point!

In the race for likes and approval, we might not be running for promotions, but we're definitely running for validation. It's easy to get sucked into this virtual rat race, where the goalposts keep shifting. Today it's about getting 50 likes on your sunset photo, but tomorrow? It's about hitting 100 on that vacation pic where you're casually meditating on a cliff (while secretly terrified of heights).

We're constantly bombarded by the lives of others—perfectly edited, filtered, and presented in the best light. And the comparison game kicks in: "Should I be doing more? Traveling more? Should my life be more... *Instagrammable*?" It's a subtle pressure, but it's there, nudging us to keep up, post more, and prove we're living our best lives.

But here's the reality: no one's life is as perfect as their feed. Behind every flawless photo is someone who probably took 20 versions before settling on the right one (and let's not even talk about the editing apps). The truth is, if we're not careful, we end up living more for the photo-op than for the actual experience. The sunsets look great on screen, but how often are we actually watching them with our own eyes, without the need to share them with the world?

Escaping this new kind of rat race means letting go of the need to constantly document and share every moment. Sure, it's fun to post and connect with friends, but when it becomes more about collecting likes than enjoying life, that's when it's time to pause. What if we started experiencing life without feeling the need to capture every second? Imagine a vacation where you didn't check your phone after every shot or a dinner where the food was eaten, not photographed.

We've all had that moment where we're too focused on getting the picture right and completely miss the actual experience. It's like being at a concert and spending the entire time recording it through your phone screen—when the best version was happening right in front of you, in real life. The concert ends, and you've got a great video but very few real memories. Where's the fun in that?

It's easy to laugh at how far we've come from those picture postcards, but maybe that's the key—laughing at the absurdity of it all. We don't have to take it so seriously. It's okay to post a photo where your hair isn't perfect or your latte art looks like an abstract painting gone wrong. Life is messy and imperfect, and that's what makes it fun. The less we try to curate a perfect image, the more real—and enjoyable—life becomes.

At the end of the day, breaking free from this kind of societal expectation means being okay with *just living*—without the need for constant external validation. It's about realizing that our value doesn't lie in the number of hearts we get on a photo but in the richness of our real, unfiltered experiences. So, go ahead—snap that photo if you must, but don't forget to actually live the moment too.

Because the best moments? They can't be captured—they can only be felt.

CHAPTER TWENTY-FOUR

Beyond the Rush: Discovering Bliss in Our Urban Sanctuary

In the bustling city life, amidst the urban chaos of Kolkata, lies a sanctuary of tranquillity we now call home. Nestled within this upscale society, I embarked on a journey with my family, steering away from the relentless race for success and the monotony of a 9-to-5 existence. It has been a year since we made this conscious choice, and our lives have taken a turn toward embracing the art of slow living.

For three decades, I danced to the tune of different time zones, navigating the highs and lows that life threw at me. Yet, deep within, there was a yearning for solitude, a desire to escape the maddening crowd and find solace in the simple joys of life. Our new home became our haven—a canvas upon which we could paint the life we had always dreamed of.

The decision to step away from the chaos was met with curiosity from some within the neighbourhood, who couldn't fathom the idea of a life without constant social engagements. Inquiries occasionally surface regarding our daily activities, and there is a tendency to presume that our preference for solitude is a cause for concern. However, we seek to convey a different narrative—one of contentment, joy, and fulfilment found within the walls of our home.

Our response to the inquisitiveness about how we spend our days is not about "passing time" but rather about living in each moment. We realized that life is not a rat race to accumulate friends, attend countless social gatherings, or relentlessly pursue wealth. It is more about savouring the beauty of each passing moment, finding joy in the little things, and relishing the company of those closest to our hearts—our family.

In a world that constantly rushes toward the next big thing, we found our rhythm in the art of slow living. We are a family that draws energy from inward existence, revelling in the peace and joy that comes from a life well-lived within the confines of our home. Our solitude is not a sentence; it's a choice—a conscious decision to find joy in the simplicity of life.

We acknowledge that this might deviate from the traditional expectation of what society generally considers a fulfilled and successful life. To those who may look at us differently for our seemingly quiet existence, I wish to convey that this is not a circumstance forced upon us. Instead, it is a carefully crafted plan, a manifestation of our desire to live life on our own terms. The universe, in its mysterious ways, presented us with an opportunity to savour the unhurried beauty of existence, and we embraced it wholeheartedly.

Not many in our neighbourhood may have noticed, but there's a beautiful water body near Ecopark, tucked away with tiny islands adorned with trees and lush greenery. These islands, covered in trees, attract thousands of migratory birds, transforming the landscape into a mesmerizing spectacle. I find immense joy in spending hours on my balcony, capturing these beautiful moments with my telephoto lens. It's a sight that truly captivates the heart.

Not far from our home lies the Kolkata airport, and from our vantage point, we can catch sight of the air traffic control tower. It's a delightful experience to witness airplanes gracefully landing or soaring into the sky. On those rare clear days, when the sky is a canvas of clarity, we are treated to the majestic sight of the revered Howrah Bridge and the nearby Vidyasagar Setu. These splendid views, although infrequent in the bustling city of Kolkata, become moments of pure joy that enhance the beauty of our daily lives.

In our busy lives, it's crucial to take a breather from time to time and care for simple things while juggling many priorities. Mindfulness is something that helps us stay sane in this chaos. The daily grind often leads to stress and health issues for many, and those who prioritize mental well-being and family are the real winners. Instead of collecting stress, we choose to aim for joy and laughter. Being a bit "selfish" about mental health is the real secret to a happier life.

At a personal level, my days are not marked by the rush to be somewhere else continuously but by the unhurried exploration of creativity. Whether it's adorning our home with the warmth of personal touches, tending to the flourishing plants in our balcony, or crafting culinary delights for our family—every moment is a celebration of life in its purest form. The therapeutic connection with nature while tending the plants brings a sense of calm in the midst of urban chaos. Cooking takes on a new meaning as the kitchen becomes a space for culinary exploration for my wife, daughter, and me. The aroma of home-cooked meals fills the air every day, not just satiating hunger but creating bonds and memories.

It's not always about going out to enjoy; it's about finding joy inwardly—in the laughter shared with loved ones and in the contentment found within oneself.

As the sun sets over our home, casting a warm glow over the landscape, I find solace in the beauty of simplicity. The view of Ecopark becomes a daily reminder that life is meant to be cherished, not rushed through. In these moments, I indulge in creative pursuits—writing, immersing myself in music, exploring art and craft, or capturing the essence of life through photography.

Author with his son Coffee

In the heart of our family beats a furry joy—our Doberman pup, a little companion who holds a special place in our daily life. We don't like to be called pet owners; we are sensible and responsible pet parents.

When we choose to stay away from the buzz of social gatherings, it's not to miss out on fun but to ensure our four-legged family member doesn't feel left alone or suffer from separation anxiety. Our home is not just a sanctuary for us but a haven for our beloved pet, who brings endless warmth to our lives.

Take New Year's Eve, for example. While the world celebrated with bursts of firecrackers, we opted for a quieter celebration, cocooned within our home. It wasn't a sacrifice; it was a conscious choice to be with our furry friend, sparing him the anxiety of loud noises. We traded the grand bash for good food, laughter, and the pure joy of our own company.

In these moments, it's not just about us; it's about creating a haven where every family member—furry or not—feels cherished. Our pet isn't just a part of the family; he is the heartbeat that adds rhythm to our days, making every choice to stay close and enjoy our own company a heartfelt one.

Our home is not a cage; it is a haven where we find joy in the unhurried pace of life. As we continue our journey in this oasis amidst the urban sprawl, I am reminded that true happiness is not found in the constant pursuit of external pleasures but in the ability to appreciate the beauty that resides within. So, let the world rush on, for in the heart of our sanctuary, we have found bliss in the art of slow living.

CHAPTER TWENTY-FIVE

Where Neither The Dreams End Nor The Thoughts Would Dry

Image by wirestock on Freepik

Stretch my wings, when I fly.
Above the clouds, up in the sky.

From there, I see all things bright,
A world of wonder in my sight.

I perch on the trees, tired when I get.
There I can see, all good things met.

When I fly long, my heart's in song,
High and far, where I belong.

Yet, when dreams fade and hopes grow thin,
I weep for the world I see within.

When I am high and far, I can see through
doors ajar.
When the goods run dry, I just simply cry.

Confused, clearing the walls with astute deft.
Should I fly the right, or turn towards the left.

Vows are many they usually share,
Fight for breath, path they dare.

They talk butter and bread for all,
Values they feel stand very tall.

Thoughts of the right, show dreams very bright.
Building castles in air, but appear out of sight.

Waking up in utter dark, seemed a lonely lark.

Today's children are the future leaders,
Living in big dreams, are tender as soft
feathers.

What they really do see,
Is it a matter of glee?

They struggle and they bleed,
In the name of religion, caste and creed.

Vying for space, path of hatred,
Dying of hunger, illusion and greed.

Hindu, muslim, rich and poor,
Can't they live together, with open door?

Who really makes the ball?
Goons, thugs whatever they call.

What happened to today's youth?
Be it from north or from the distant south.

Always I find them glued to the telly,
Left with no desire burning in their belly.

Strolling down the mall with a pricey cell,
Life without which seems like a living hell.

Little do they realize, the need of the hour.
Neglecting vital issues, sitting in ivory tower.

Cricket is like a national religion,
Pushing all else to solitary oblivion.

Every time the little master fails,
The entire nation sobs and wails.

Let there be one man with imagination,
Rather a whole bunch lying under illusion.

Often appearing on the telli in Gandhian attire,
Speaking on issues which becomes a satire.
Do they have the knowledge or the right desire?

Promises they never fulfil, neither do they care.
Let there one man with visions to share,
New beliefs and dreams that he deems to dare.

Let it be this man who values it to be an Indian,
Uniting us all within the cord of national union.

That time is not very far away,
When I simply wake up a day.
Finding things just as right as they say,
Prejudices of colour and tongue all I can allay.

The nation will emerge stronger from this ordeal,
And all will work together with vigour and zeal.

I will again fly so high and high in the sky,
Where neither the dreams end nor the thoughts would dry.

CHAPTER TWENTY-SIX

Your Next Chapter: A Reflection

So, what's your next chapter? Take a moment to dream. If you weren't limited by the expectations of others, what would you do? What passions have you left unexplored? Think about something that excites you—no matter how small or how wild it seems.

Maybe it's that sketch you always wanted to try but never picked up the pencil for, write a book about your life experiences, or perhaps you've fantasized about running a marathon—despite the fact that your current idea of exercise is carrying the cup of tea from kitchen counter to your study table. Whatever it is, give yourself permission to explore it.

Write it down. Well, writing something down might feel a bit cliché, but trust me, it's like planting a seed. Let yourself imagine what that dream might look like if you gave it space to grow. Whether it's starting a new hobby, learning something new, or taking a completely different direction in life—this is your chance to shape the path ahead. The possibilities are endless, and they're yours to discover.

Think about what that dream might look like if you gave it room to grow. Will you start a gardening club? Become the next great novelist? Or maybe even launch a YouTube channel about your pet's day-to-day adventures.

It doesn't have to be perfect or grand. You might try your hand at baking and set off the smoke alarm (it can happen to the best of us), but at least you'll have a laugh and a story to tell.

Escaping the rat race isn't the end of the story. It's the beginning of something far more exciting—a life that's truly yours.

CHAPTER TWENTY-SEVEN

A Personal Anecdote: My Life Beyond the Rat Race

Now, let me share a little slice of my own journey beyond the rat race. After managing the product development for a global brand raking in nearly $700 million, you'd think I'd be basking in the glory of my success, right? Wrong! Instead, I find myself at home, hearing my wife call out, "Bhaater maar ta gele dao, cha ta dile na?, ekhane ektu dhulo hoye geche—porishkar kora dorkar, machine e kapor ta diye dao, dishwasher ta chaliye dao!" (Translation: "Sieve the rice starch and don't forget the tea; it's gotten a bit dusty here—it needs cleaning; place the laundry inside the washer; get the utensils inside the dishwasher!")

Ah yes, the transition from a corporate leader to the designated "domestic engineer" has been quite the ride! Here I was, thinking I'd traded the daily grind for a life of freedom, only to realize I had unwittingly entered a different kind of rat race—the race to clean the house before my wife notices the *undertakers of dust* plotting their takeover in the corners!

Picture me, a former high-flying professional, now wielding a broom like a sword, battling against invisible dust while occasionally feeling a pang of irritation: "How on earth did she manage all this before?!" And let's be honest, some days I feel surprised — as I discover a mountain of laundry that's mysteriously multiplied overnight.

But you know what? Amidst the chaos, I'm learning to enjoy life on my own terms. Each dusting session has turned into a mini-adventure, and every pile of laundry? A new quest! Who knew that taking the plunge into domestic bliss could be so entertaining? So, while I may not be raking in millions at the office anymore, I'm definitely rich in laughter and peace —and isn't that what life is all about?

About The Author

Sudip Chowdhury was born and raised in the Eastern part of India. He went onto pursuing a master's degree in mechanical engineering from one of the most prestigious technical universities in Europe.

Over the years, Sudip has worked with several prominent companies and gained broad experience in product development across a variety of sectors, including plastic toys, servo hydraulics, process industry bearings, and industrial gearbox. His history in engineering leadership is extensive, and he has successfully led teams in countries like India and Hong Kong.

Sudip is passionate about working with people and building meaningful relationships. As a trained coach and facilitative leader, he firmly believes in developing high-performance teams that are collaborative, supportive, and focused on achieving shared goals. Through his extensive industry experience and leadership skills, he offers valuable insights and practical advice to aspiring professionals looking to make it big in the corporate world.

Outside of work, he enjoys reading, cooking, photography and traveling. He is known to be a role model for aspiring engineers.